GUIDING WORD

VOLUME 1

The Books of
Moses

CONCORDIA PUBLISHING HOUSE · SAINT LOUIS

Library of Congress Cataloging-in-Publication Data

Title: The Books of Moses : guiding word.

Description: Saint Louis : Concordia Publishing House, 2024- | Series: The guiding word ; volume 1 | Summary: "This six-volume series will take readers through each book of the Bible, showing the unified narrative of God's plan of salvation. Using this resource, readers will (1) understand the history of God's people and His promise; (2) gain a basic grasp of each book of the Bible; (3) see Jesus' saving mission in each book of the Bible; and (4) develop fundamental Bible reading and interpretation skills"-- Provided by publisher.

Identifiers: LCCN 2022060172 (print) | LCCN 2022060173 (ebook) | ISBN 9780758671882 (v. 1 ; paperback) | ISBN 9780758671899 (v. 1 ; ebook)

Subjects: LCSH: Bible Old Testament--Introductions.

Classification: LCC BS1140.3 .B66 2024 (print) | LCC BS1140.3 (ebook) | DDC 221.6--dc23/eng/20230621

LC record available at https://lccn.loc.gov/2022060172

LC ebook record available at https://lccn.loc.gov/2022060173

1 2 3 4 5 6 7 8 9 10   33 32 31 30 29 28 27 26 25 24

TABLE OF CONTENTS

Welcome

Welcome to *Guiding Word*. This six-volume collection will help you better read and understand the Bible, the most important book ever written. In it, we read and hear God's Word, which is written so that we may believe that Jesus is the Christ, and that by believing we may have eternal life in His name (John 20:31).

Why have another Bible resource? First, the Bible is a complex library of books, and it is often intimidating for people to read on their own. Second, while there are many resources designed to help you read and understand the Bible, each has its own format and style and may not be suitable for every learner. We hope this resource will fill a gap and be useful for you.

Think of this series of books as a travel guide to the Bible. Just as a travel guide helps you prepare for and better enjoy a trip, this resource will enable you to better understand and appreciate the Bible as you journey through it. The sections have been designed to help you prepare for reading and understanding difficult passages, to explain the overall course of the Scriptures, to prompt you to reflect on the text as you read, to point out important milestones and events, and to guide you to Jesus' presence throughout the Bible.

If you are already familiar with the organization of the Bible, feel free to skip ahead to the section titled "What's in *Guiding Word*?"

What's in the Bible?

The Bible is all about God's plan to restore fallen humanity and His broken creation by sending His Son. But what's in the Bible? How do we look at it? How do we use it? Though we call the Bible a book, it's actually a collection of sixty-six books. These were written over a period of 1,500 years by many authors.

The Bible has two divisions: the Old Testament and the New Testament. We don't use the word *testament* too often today. It's related to words like *covenant* and *contract*.

The Old Testament includes the first thirty-nine books of the Bible. These are the books written about the events that happened before Jesus was born. They all point us toward Jesus. The name *Old Testament* is a little misleading because sometimes we think of old things as not important or out of style. Instead, these books can be thought of as the first covenant or promise that God made to His people to send the Savior, Jesus. And as you will see, Jesus is present throughout the Old Testament. The New Testament includes the last twenty-seven books of the Bible, which record Jesus' life and mission, as well as the life of Jesus' early followers in the church. These books point us back to Jesus and how He fulfilled all of God's promises made for us in the Old Testament. Again, these are all about Jesus.

The books of the Bible are organized in a way that may seem confusing at first but makes sense when you know the system. How are the books in a library organized? In libraries, books are organized by their type. Fiction is in one section, and nonfiction is in another; magazines are in one spot and children's books in another. The same goes for the Bible. Instead of the books being ordered by the date they were written or by their authors, the books of the Bible are put in categories, or genres; then the books are generally organized by date written within that genre.

NAVIGATING THE LIBRARY

The first five books of the Old Testament—Genesis, Exodus, Leviticus, Numbers, and Deuteronomy—are called the Books of Moses, or the Torah, meaning "Law of God." They were written down by Moses and are covered in the first volume of this series.

The next books in the Old Testament are called the Books of History. These tell the history of God's people from the time of Moses up to the time of Jesus and are covered in the second volume.

Next are the Books of Wisdom and Poetry. These poetical books were written at different times during the Old Testament history, mostly by kings David and Solomon. These are covered in the third volume.

The last group of Old Testament books are the Books of the Prophets. These books record God's special messages to His Old Testament people, mostly during the second half of their history. They are discussed in the fourth volume.

The New Testament has five genres. The first four books—Matthew, Mark, Luke, and John—are called the Gospels. Each Gospel tells of the life and mission of Jesus from a different writer and perspective. These accounts make up the heart of the Bible and are covered in the fifth *Guiding Word* volume.

Next is the book of the Acts of the Apostles (also known simply as Acts). This historical book records events from the early years of the Christian Church and the lives of the first Christians after Jesus ascended into heaven. The next books are called the Pauline Epistles (*epistle* means "letter"). These are letters that the apostle Paul wrote to the early Christians. Near the end of the New Testament are the General Epistles. These are letters that other people besides Paul wrote to the early Christians. The final book of the Bible is the only book of prophecy in the New Testament, the book of Revelation. This shows the vision Jesus revealed to the apostle John about life in the end times (that is, the time between Christ's first and second coming) and the restoration of God's creation. The books of Acts through Revelation are covered in the sixth and final volume of *Guiding Word*.

66 BOOKS OF THE BIBLE

OLD TESTAMENT	GENESIS
	EXODUS
BOOKS OF	LEVITICUS
MOSES	NUMBERS
(Torah)	DEUTERONOMY
	JOSHUA
	JUDGES
	RUTH
	1 SAMUEL
	2 SAMUEL
HISTORY	1 KINGS
	2 KINGS
	1 CHRONICLES
	2 CHRONICLES
	EZRA
	NEHEMIAH
	ESTHER
	JOB
WISDOM	PSALMS
& POETRY	PROVERBS
	ECCLESIASTES
	SONG OF SOLOMON
	ISAIAH
	JEREMIAH
	LAMENTATIONS
	EZEKIEL
	DANIEL
	HOSEA
	JOEL
	AMOS
PROPHETS	OBADIAH
	JONAH
	MICAH
	NAHUM
	HABAKKUK
	ZEPHANIAH
	HAGGAI
	ZECHARIAH
	MALACHI
NEW TESTAMENT	MATTHEW
	MARK
GOSPELS	LUKE
	JOHN
HISTORY	ACTS
	ROMANS
	1 CORINTHIANS
	2 CORINTHIANS
	GALATIANS
	EPHESIANS
	PHILIPPIANS
PAULINE	COLOSSIANS
EPISTLES	1 THESSALONIANS
(Letters)	2 THESSALONIANS
	1 TIMOTHY
	2 TIMOTHY
	TITUS
	PHILEMON
	HEBREWS
	JAMES
	1 PETER
GENERAL	2 PETER
EPISTLES	1 JOHN
	2 JOHN
	3 JOHN
	JUDE
END TIMES	REVELATION

Navigating the Bible

When you open up a Bible, you'll see chapter and verse numbers scattered throughout the pages. Did you know that those numbers were not originally there? As people used the Bible more and more and made copies, later scholars eventually put in these numbers to help people quickly find sections or passages. We call these Bible references.

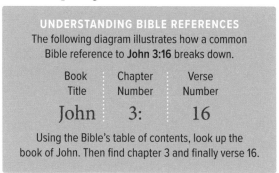

UNDERSTANDING BIBLE REFERENCES

The following diagram illustrates how a common Bible reference to **John 3:16** breaks down.

Book Title	Chapter Number	Verse Number
John	3:	16

Using the Bible's table of contents, look up the book of John. Then find chapter 3 and finally verse 16.

What's in *Guiding Word*?

Each volume of *Guiding Word* is laid out in a similar fashion. After this series introduction is an introduction for that specific volume. Then, each book of the Bible has its own introduction, which will help you better understand and dig into that particular book.

Each book of the Bible follows an outline, which breaks the book into major divisions and then each division into sections. The section heads were not included in the original biblical text but were added later to help clarify how the text flows from narrative to narrative or idea to idea. In *Guiding Word*, these correspond to the subheadings in the ESV translation of the Bible. From here on out, we will refer to these subhead sections as "passages."

Following the pattern of a travel guide, *Guiding Word* includes some features to help you read through, better understand, and reflect on each passage of the Bible. These features include the following:

(1) **Orientation.** This is a short summary of each passage. Just as a travel guide gives you a glimpse of where you will be going on your journey before you arrive, the summary will help orient you to where you are in the Bible and where you are going. After reading the summary for each passage, read the text itself in your Bible. Alternatively, if you are skimming a book of the Bible, previewing the book, or only want to understand the high points before reading deeper, these summaries are a good place to start.

(2) **Observation Points.** In the side margins, you will find open-ended questions. Use these reflection questions to help you slow down, observe, and reflect on the passage. There is room in the side margin for recording reflections, thoughts, and notes as you go. Just as a travel guide will prompt you to look out for specific things on your way, the reflection questions will help you better observe what's going on in the text.

(3) Landmarks. These special features, interspersed in the text, will help you appreciate the overall journey through God's Word. In any journey, you will encounter landmarks of all types that pop out to you, may interest you, or may even make you scratch your head. Landmarks in *Guiding Word* are identified by icons and colored bars, and can be read before or after you read the corresponding passage. Landmarks include the following categories:

VISUALIZE

This feature includes maps, diagrams, pictures, or infographics to help you visualize scenes, locations, and concepts in a passage.

PICTURE OF THE SAVIOR

This Old Testament feature highlights people, places, or events that set the stage for the coming of Jesus and help reveal His work of salvation.

LINK BETWEEN THE TESTAMENTS

In the Old Testament, this Landmark highlights people or events that Jesus or His apostles will discuss, explain, or fulfill in the New Testament. In the New Testament, this feature points the reader back to the Old Testament person or event that set the stage for the New Testament passage.

CLEAR THE CONFUSION

This Landmark clarifies passages that are likely to leave the reader confused and fills the gaps—providing backstories, describing future developments, or discussing the significance of the event.

SET THE SCENE

This feature explains important cultural or historical themes that help you better understand the context of the passage.

WAYPOINT

This feature is designed to be a longer stopping point. When you travel, you will likely stop at notable locations for an extended period of time to really experience the destination. Waypoints in *Guiding Word* function like stopping points that are worth investigating along the journey through God's Word. Each Waypoint has a three-part structure:

- What does this text show us?

- What does this text reveal about God's plan of salvation?

- What does this text uncover about our identity and calling as God's people today?

Each Waypoint also has reflection questions associated with it. The Waypoints can be considered on your own or in a group study. However you choose to use the Waypoints is up to you, but use the summaries and reflection prompts to help guide you through a deeper reading of the text.

How to Use *Guiding Word*

You can use this resource in multiple ways:

- Read through the Bible on your own, passage by passage. The summary of each passage will help orient you to where the narrative is taking you, and the reflection questions are observation prompts that will help you pay closer attention to what you're reading. The interspersed Landmark features will help you visualize important images or concepts, or understand and connect key themes to the overall story of the Scriptures.

- Read through the Bible in a small group or Bible study setting. The guided summaries and reflection questions make good prompts if you are reading through the Scriptures as a group, providing some reflections along the way. The Waypoint sections also serve as great places to stop and reflect on key narratives.

- Read a good thirty-thousand-foot summary of the Bible. *Guiding Word* includes summaries of passages, and if you have never read certain books of the Bible or are intimidated by their length, you can take a few minutes to get introduced or oriented to them via summaries and graphics.

Whether or not you've read through all or parts of the Bible before, *Guiding Word* will serve as your companion and guide through the journey.

The Books of Moses

The first five books of the Old Testament are called the Books of Moses, as they have traditionally been ascribed to Moses. Other names for this group are the Pentateuch (meaning "five books" in Greek) or the Torah (meaning "law" or "testimony" in Hebrew). Most of these books were likely written down by Moses during the wilderness wanderings of God's people. The final section of the final book, Deuteronomy, was likely completed by a scholar (possibly Joshua) after Moses' death.

These books are significant for many reasons. Not only do they tell of the beginning of the world but they also lay down the narrative of God's first called family, from Abraham, and trace their lineage all the way through the exodus to the very borders of the Promised

Land. Many of the Old Testament narratives that are the most popular among Christians—including Adam and Eve, Cain and Abel, the flood, the tower of Babel, Abraham and Isaac, Jacob and Esau, Joseph, Moses, the golden calf, and manna in the wilderness—are all contained in these five books. These books are also significant because they record God's laws for His Old Testament people: all the civil and ceremonial laws by which they were to form their nation and the moral law, God's commands for what is right and wrong for all people, which are passed along in the Ten Commandments. Importantly, these books also give us the promises of the Christ. God first promised the coming Messiah in Genesis 3:15, right after the fall into sin. The rest of the Books of Moses track the generations of God's people from that first promise, through Abraham and his family, down to Moses leading God's people out of slavery in Egypt. The promise of the Messiah is the clear thread that weaves its way through the Books of Moses.

Journeying through the Books of Moses

Taking the journey though these first five books of the Bible can feel like a wild ride. Genesis is mostly narrative, meaning that reading through it can feel like following a multigenerational story. The first half of Exodus, the second book, picks up four hundred years after the end of Genesis and describes God rescuing His people from Egypt. The second half of the book mostly outlines God's instructions to Moses about His laws and instructions for worship while the Israelites were camped at Mount Sinai. The third book, Leviticus, describes the worship laws God continued to give at Mount Sinai, notably about the Levites, and reads quite differently from the other books. Numbers then picks up the action with God's people leaving Mount Sinai and details their lives in the wilderness as well as other laws and instructions God gave at that time. Deuteronomy is mostly a series of farewell sermons that Moses gave the people while on the border of the Promised Land.

These varied forms have often led people to frustration when attempting to read through the Bible for the first time. The second half of Exodus or the book of Leviticus can feel more like an instruction manual than anything else. Know that these details in these varied forms all help flesh out the life of God's people as He formed them for His purposes. You do not have to spend equal time reading through and considering all the passages of Scripture. As you journey through God's Word, find comfort in how each part paints a picture of God's plan of salvation in different ways.

The Books of Moses, with Their General Divisions

- **Genesis**
  - The Book of the Ancients (1:1–11:26)
  - The Book of the Patriarchs (11:27–36:43)
  - The Book of Joseph (37:1–50:26)

- **Exodus**
  - Israel Enslaved in Egypt (1:1–11:10)
  - Passover and Exodus (12:1–15:21)
  - Through the Wilderness to Mount Sinai (15:22–18:27)
  - Events at Mount Sinai (19:1–24:18)
  - Directions for the Tabernacle and Accessories (25:1–31:18)
  - Apostasy and Restoration (32:1–34:35)
  - Construction of the Tabernacle (35:1–40:38)

- **Leviticus**
  - Manual of Offerings (1:1–7:38)
  - Ordination into the Priesthood (8:1–10:20)
  - Manual of Purity (11:1–15:33)
  - The Day of Atonement (16:1–34)
  - Showing Reverence for the Sanctuary (17:1–22:33)
  - Observing the Sabbath (23:1–27:34)

- **Numbers**
  - From Mount Sinai to the Promised Land (1:1–6:27)
  - Consecrating the Tabernacle (7:1–12:16)
  - From the Promised Land to the Wilderness (13:1–14:45)
  - Religious Questions (15:1–19:22)
  - Journey Back toward the Promised Land (20:1–21:35)
  - Preparing to Enter the Promised Land (22:1–25:18)
  - The Second Census and New Laws (26:1–27:23)
  - God Confirms Offering Practices (28:1–30:16)
  - The Defeat of Midian (31:1–32:42)
  - The Final Preparations (33:1–36:13)

- **Deuteronomy**
  - Historical Prologue (1:1–4:43)
  - Reviewing the Covenant (4:44–23:14)
  - Miscellaneous Laws (23:15–28:68)
  - Renewing the Covenant (29:1–30:20)
  - Leadership Succession (31:1–34:12)

GENESIS

Welcome to Genesis

Genesis, meaning "beginnings," is a powerful book that lays the foundation for everything else in the Bible. It tells the story of creation, the first humans, the fall into sin, the flood, Abraham, Isaac, Jacob, Joseph, and so many other accounts central to the life of faith. It tells of the human condition, the origins of sin and death, and God's faithfulness to His chosen people throughout the first generations of humanity. Most importantly, it points us to God's promise to rescue and restore humanity through our Lord Jesus Christ and shows how God preserved that promise throughout the ages. Dive in to read, enjoy, and contemplate these amazing accounts of our first ancestors and God's fidelity to them and to us through the promised Messiah.

What are your first impressions of Genesis? What narratives or images come to your mind when you reflect on this book? What are some specific things you'd like to learn more about?

Genesis at a Glance

- **Start:** Genesis begins at the very creation of the world.

- **End:** Genesis ends with the death of Joseph, around 1804 BC.

- **Theme:** Genesis tracks the passing of the promise of God's Savior from generation to generation, beginning with the first humans, through Israel, and to all nations.

- **Author and Date:** The prophet Moses wrote Genesis, likely between 1446 BC and 1406 BC.

- **Places Visited:** The Garden of Eden, Mesopotamia, Canaan, Egypt

- **Journey Time:** The fifty books of Genesis can be read in about three and a half hours.

- **Outline:**
  - The Book of the Ancients (1:1–11:26)
  - The Book of the Patriarchs (11:27–36:43)
  - The Book of Joseph (37:1–50:26)

Five Top Sights and Spectacles of Genesis

The Creation, Fall, and Promise (1:1–3:24) Watch as God creates all things, with humans as the special creation. Witness the first humans rebel against God, and marvel at God's promise to raise up a descendant of Eve to one day destroy the power of the fallen angel who led mankind into temptation and the fall.

The Flood (6:1–9:29) Observe how mankind deserts God and His plan of salvation and becomes more and more evil, and study how God preserves a remnant of faithful people through Noah, his family, and the animals in the massive ship of the ark.

God Calls Abram (12:1–9; 15:1–21) See how God chooses one man from the line of Adam and Eve to bear a special promise. Ponder how God blesses Abram and promises to faithfully preserve his family for the sake of the Messiah.

Jacob's Travels (27:1–29:35) Scrutinize the deep dysfunctions of the descendants of Abram as they scheme and deceive one another. Examine God's faithfulness to preserve His promise and His people in their brokenness.

Joseph Forgives His Brothers (44:1–46:34) Discover the depths of God's power as Joseph forgives his brothers of great evil. Rejoice with Jacob's family as they are reunited and saved from starvation and death.

Seeing Jesus in Genesis

When you think of the book of Genesis, does Jesus come to mind? Why or why not?

Though people often think of the creation of the world, the flood, or the account of Joseph in Egypt as the center of Genesis, the book actually focuses on God's promise to preserve His people despite their sin and rebellion. Starting with the first promise of the Messiah in Genesis 3:15, and then moving throughout the narratives of the book, Genesis follows successive generations of the family of Adam and Eve, who carry the promise that one of their descendants will destroy the serpent's power and bless the world. As you read of these often very flawed generations in the book, keep an eye out for God's faithfulness to preserve this family. In addition, look for mentions of the Angel of the Lord, who shows up at critical times (like at the sacrifice of Isaac). Most interpreters see these as appearances of the Son of God before He took on human flesh. He is there throughout the narrative, guiding and guarding His people as they await His coming in the flesh.

The Book of the Ancients (1:1–11:26)

The first eleven chapters of Genesis lay down the earliest foundations of what will happen in the Bible. They establish who God is, the creation, mankind's fall into sin, and God's faithfulness to preserve His people despite their sins. Great time periods and critical events are quickly covered in a few chapters.

THE CREATION OF THE WORLD (1:1–31)

 WAYPOINT

What does this text show us?
The Scriptures begin with an epic account of the beginning of the world. Over six days, God creates all things, forming the earth and all its inhabitants, calling them good. On the sixth day, God creates man and woman, His special creation, calling them very good. They are made in God's image, reflecting God's character and acting as God's representatives in the world.

What does this text reveal about God's plan of salvation?
From the very beginning of creation, God is in control. Though not every detail is spelled out, this much is clear: He creates and orders all things. This is not done in a chaotic and brutal fashion, as many proponents of evolution propose, but by God's Word, from nothing, according to God's design. God the Holy Trinity is also seen here: the Father, the Word (the Son of God), and the Spirit.

What does this text uncover about our identity and calling as God's people today?
Contrary to so much that is taught in the world, creation is no accident. All things are designed and created by the Creator. Because of sin, the perfect creation has been corrupted, but that does not mean that creation has no design or purpose. God creates humanity to care for all creation. That is our God-given purpose—to be fruitful and fill the earth, and to manage, enjoy, and explore that which God has created.

What does the ordering of the days of creation show us about who God is and what His intention is for creation?

God cares about His creation. What does that mean about how we should care for creation as well?

What is one way you can be a better steward of creation?

Contemplate the picture of the light first shining on the unformed earth. Especially consider the Holy Spirit hovering over the waters. What does it mean to you to call the Holy Spirit "the Lord and giver of life" in the Nicene Creed?

Imagine descending from heaven with Jesus, His angel armies, and all the saints, preparing to stand upon the new earth in your risen, glorified body. What would you see, feel, and hear?

VISUALIZE

In six days, God formed a beautiful home perfectly suited for us humans and all the creatures that share it with us. Though it is no longer perfect today, we can catch glimpses of its original majesty and grandeur when we watch waves pound on the ocean shore, walk through a forest, or gaze at a mountain range.

As we begin Genesis 1, with the Spirit of God hovering over the waters, it is valuable to spend a few moments pondering God's newly created world because God promises He will create new heavens and a new earth on the day Christ returns. With risen, glorified bodies, we will forever enjoy a new home where suffering and pain will never strike us, and dying and death will flee away forever.

Day One

In Genesis 1:3, God said, "Let there be light." Instantly, light pierced the darkness, illuminating the earth, which was covered with water. The sun, moon, and stars will not be created until the fourth day, so this was a special light God set in place to separate the day from the night. But already God was establishing time, and the sequence of night and day, sleep and activity that would guide the lives of His human creatures.

Day Two

On the second day, God spread an expanse that separated the waters on the surface of the earth beneath from the waters high overhead. Within this clear expanse of sky, all kinds of birds, insects, and other creatures will fly. Soft, billowy clouds provided shade and brought water for the earth.

Day Three

On the third day, God gathered the waters together to bring forth dry land where we can live and move. With a word, He commanded the earth to bring forth vegetation; a wide variety of plants spread and covered the earth. The diversity of plant life that fills the earth is staggering. The colors and textures of plants please our eyes, while the aromas and flavors of this plant life—such as grains, fruits, vegetables, and spices—provide us humans and other creatures a delicious variety of tastes and smells to enjoy as food.

Day Four

Beginning on the fourth day, God filled in and refined the things He created on the first three days. On day four, He enhanced the light He created on the first day. He placed the sun, moon, and stars in the sky to give light to the earth day and night. Not only did the sun produce heat for the earth, but it also provided light to make the plants grow in all their wide variety. The moon controls the ocean tides and its phases help us measure time. The stars and the constellations also help us to measure the yearly cycle.

Day Five

On the second day, God created the sky, separating the waters below from those above. Three days later, on the fifth day, God created fish and invertebrates of all kinds and sizes. These animals fill the oceans, lakes, and rivers. He also created birds and all manner of flying creatures to fill the skies. When we ponder the incredible variety and beauty of the flying and swimming creatures and all the special abilities God has given them, we see His wisdom and His power, and we marvel at how He designed His creatures to live together in perfect peace and harmony.

Day Six

On the third day, God made the dry land appear. On the sixth day, He created the animals that live on the earth—wild beasts, domesticated animals, and those that creep and crawl across the earth. Finally, with all these in place, God created man and woman in His image, giving them the charge to rule over the earth, not as masters to abuse the creatures set below them but as His representatives, using their talent, intelligence, and skill to make the earth more fruitful and hospitable for every creature who shares it.

Day Seven

Finally, the seventh day arrived. God's work of creating the heavens and the earth was complete. He looked at all that He had made and was well pleased. The earth and all its creatures lived in perfect harmony under the kind, caring, benevolent hand of humanity. God rested from His creating labor, setting a pattern for human activity. Six days of work, followed by a day of rest. On that day, we rest from our daily labors  and gather together in His presence to let Him serve us, remind us of our spiritual needs, and anticipate our future home when He will make the present heavens and earth pass away and replace them with a heavens and earth that will be permanent and glorious, full of life and beauty forever.

The Seventh Day, God Rests (2:1–3)

On the seventh day of creation, God rests, establishing the seven-day cycle of the week. By resting, God establishes not only His holy Sabbath day for His people but also the gift of rest.

The Creation of Man and Woman (2:4–24)

Genesis now takes us back to day six and the creation of man and woman, going into more detail. God first forms the man's body from the earth, then breathes into his nostrils the breath of life. Adam becomes a living creature.

Next, God plants a garden called Eden for Adam's home. It is filled with all kinds of fruit trees for Adam's food. Adam's work is to tend and keep the garden.

God brings the animals to Adam so he can name them. But among the animals, Adam finds no suitable helper. So God puts Adam in a deep sleep, takes a rib from his side, and uses it to form Eve, the special partner for Adam. God unites them as husband and wife, establishing His good pattern for marriage and family. God tells them to care for and have dominion over His creation

Take a moment and really examine this narrative. What details stick out to you as you read this? Why do they stick out to you?

CLEAR THE CONFUSION

Where exactly was the Garden of Eden?

The Bible cites some rather specific details about the location of the region of Eden in which God planted the garden. Specifically, the Bible notes two familiar river names among the four, the Tigris and the Euphrates. Though these and other details seem to locate Eden somewhere in the region of Mesopotamia, we are unsure as to its exact location. The worldwide flood, which is described in Genesis 6–9, most certainly changed worldwide geography, including the course of rivers. In the end, all speculation of the exact topography and location of Eden on a map is futile.

From the descriptions in the Bible, imagine what it might have been like to live in the Garden of Eden. What would you have seen, heard, felt, and done if you were there before the fall?

PICTURE OF THE SAVIOR

Adam

Complementary colors draw each other out in a picture, and in the same way, Adam intensifies the colors of Jesus' character by contrast. Before he sinned, Adam was the ideal man in every sense of the phrase. He existed in loving communion with God in the Garden of Eden, and death did not exist in the "very good" creation God had made. When Adam and his wife ate the forbidden fruit, however, sin entered humanity as a terminal, hereditary illness for every human born thereafter. Through one man, all were condemned and sentenced to death. God knew exactly what He would do in response: send His one and only Son to live one life that would atone for the sins of all. Though we were split from God's side by the despicable act of the first Adam, we have been reunited in faith by the glorious act of the Second Adam, Jesus Christ.

The Fall (3:1–24)

 WAYPOINT

What does this text show us?

The fallen angel Satan, either possessing or in the form of a serpent, enters into Eden and tempts Adam and Eve to disobey and rebel against God. They do so by eating the fruit God had commanded them not to eat. With this act of defiance, sin and death enter the world. God drives Adam and Eve out from the garden but first curses Satan. God promises that one day an offspring of Eve would crush Satan's head. This is the first promise of the Messiah in the Scriptures.

What stands out to you about the interactions among Adam, Eve, Satan, and God in this section?

What does this text reveal about God's plan of salvation?

This section of the Scriptures sets not only the plot for the rest of the Bible but also the whole course of human history. We see God creating good rules for His human creatures, giving them the freedom to love Him in their actions by obeying His rule. We see the first appearance of Satan, leader of the fallen angels, entering into creation and tempting the first humans to rebel against God's good rule. We see the disobedience and how suffering and death enter creation. Mankind's perfect relationship with God is broken. All humans will now be born with original sin, an innate tendency to sin. The consequences of this rebellion include increased pain and sorrow in childbearing, struggle for survival, and ultimately death. But we also see God's promise of a Savior. An offspring of Adam and Eve would one day crush Satan's power. This would be the Messiah, Jesus, a descendant of Adam and Eve, who would fulfill that promise. On the cross and in the empty tomb, Jesus would reverse that which Satan tempted Adam and Eve to do. By His obedience, Jesus gives the forgiveness of the sin of rebellion against God and grants a new eternal life to God's people.

What details from this section reveal the nature of sin and God's response to the fallen creation?

How have you seen the effects of the fallen creation in the world around you? What do you think it will be like when Jesus returns to make all things new?

What does this text uncover about our identity and calling as God's people today?

It cannot be understated just how important this third chapter is to understanding everything. In a few lines, we see the cause of brokenness and suffering in this world; namely, rebellion against God, which leads to death. We also see God's promise to not abandon His creation to death, even though Adam and Eve do not deserve God's saving. Unlike Adam and Eve, we do not have to look forward to the time when the Promised One would come. Jesus has already come for us and has taken away Satan's power to accuse us. By faith in Christ, we are God's children now and we will be given a new Eden when Jesus returns one day to raise the dead and make all things new.

 CLEAR THE CONFUSION

What's going on with the serpent?

As expected, the serpent was a slippery character in the account of the fall. What we know about the serpent can be extracted from the surrounding text of Genesis. First, the serpent was as the Bible says: a serpent. Moses' account does not indicate an allegorical or representative interpretation of the serpent's true identity. When the serpent began to speak to Eve, something supernatural or otherworldly occurred, according to the previous chapters. In chapter 2, when God brought all the animals to Adam, the serpent was determined to be unsuitable as a helper for him, clearly inferior and unable to communicate with him. Moreover, God deemed the serpent "good" along with the rest of creation, so it wouldn't make sense for the serpent itself to tempt Eve into sin. From the surrounding evidence, we can conclude that an outside, evil force must have used the serpent to turn the first man and woman away from God. The account of Job gives the name of a notorious tempter in the Bible: Satan, the Adversary. Other passages in the Scriptures (1 Kings 22:20–23; 2 Peter 2:4; Jude 6) point us to a fallen angel who is the tempting culprit. Satan, therefore, is our logical suspect. As the fallen angel who deeply desires God's great love (humanity) to turn away from Him, Satan used the wily serpent as an instrument to turn the desires of Adam and Eve into themselves.

LINK BETWEEN THE TESTAMENTS

**Through One Man, Death → Through Another, New Life
(Genesis 3 → Romans 5:12–21)**

At this moment, paradise was lost. The simplest of acts—one man and one woman, eating one fruit in defiance of God—gouged a deep divide between man and God, who created him, and it condemned him to death. Sin metastasized and persisted in the human heart of each following generation, tainting God's once-perfect world with all manner of suffering and evil. Yet, as Paul remarks,

> Therefore, as one trespass led to condemnation for all men, so one act of righteousness leads to justification and life for all men. For as by the one man's disobedience the many were made sinners, so by the one man's obedience the many will be made righteous. Now the law came in to increase the trespass, but where sin increased, grace abounded all the more, so that, as sin reigned in death, grace also might reign through righteousness leading to eternal life through Jesus Christ our Lord. (Romans 5:18–21)

Jesus came as the Second Adam, the one who, by His death and resurrection, would cover the sins of the world in His precious blood to restore mankind to God, who loves us dearly.

CAIN AND ABEL (4:1–26)

 WAYPOINT

What does this text show us?
Adam and Eve, now outside the Garden of Eden, have children. Cain, the oldest son of Adam and Eve, grows furious that God favored his brother Abel's sacrifice over his. Despite God's warning, Cain murders his brother. God reveals His mercy and character by protecting Cain with a mark and letting him go, despite Cain's grievous sin. Unrepentant, Cain rejects God's promise, and his descendants would share his unbelief and violence.

What does this text reveal about God's plan of salvation?
The name Eve gave her oldest son, *Cain* (which means "gotten"), hints that she may have believed him to be the promised Messiah. Yet he was the first person to commit murder. In Cain and his descendants, we see the great division between all people: those who have faith in God's promises and those who reject them. Even so, God shows Cain mercy, revealing both God's justice and mercy. Though God would continue to enact His wrath against sins, He would have patience with His faithful people as they waited

 What is the relationship between God and humanity like after the fall?

 What is significant about blood in this section? How is that seen elsewhere in the Bible?

the coming of the true Messiah, Jesus, who would appear many thousands of years later from the line of Seth, the descendant who would replace Cain in the line of the Messiah.

What does this text uncover about our identity and calling as God's people today?
We all inherit original sin from our parents. Though we might not commit murder like Cain did, the effects of our brokenness corrupt every aspect of our lives. Sin is always lurking at the doors of our hearts. In Jesus, we receive God's mercy, and in Cain, we see a pale reflection of God sparing us from the justice we deserve for our sins. As we live each day as God's chosen people in Christ, we, too, are to watch for lurking temptations to sin and hurt those whom God has put in our paths.

In what ways do God's words to Cain apply to our lives today?

Adam's Descendants to Noah (5:1–32)

Genesis then traces Adam's believing descendants through Seth down to Noah and his three sons. These descendants have tremendously long life spans, which begin to diminish sharply in the generations after the flood.

 CLEAR THE CONFUSION

How might humans have lived for so long before the flood?

The Scriptures don't give us a reason for the large disparity between pre-flood and post-flood life spans, but we can infer that the earth's climate must have changed drastically as a result of the flood's devastation. A very different climate could produce different living environments that are much less supportive of an elongated human life span.

As you read this, imagine what life might have been like on earth during this time. Why did things get so bad?

Increasing Corruption on Earth (6:1–8)

The sons of God (descendants of believing Seth) take for wives the daughters of men (daughters of unbelieving Cain) and are drawn from the faith. They will be known as the Nephilim, or tyrants of the earth. God gives mankind 120 years before He will blot them and the animals from the face of the earth.

Noah and the Flood (6:9–7:24)

By God's grace, Noah finds favor before God. God warns him to build an ark, a large boat, to save his family and representatives of the birds and land animals from the coming flood, which will destroy all mankind.

CLEAR THE CONFUSION

What does Genesis 6:5 have to do with the flood and my life today?

This verse explains why God decided to destroy mankind through a devastating flood. What was the extent of the evil within humans? "Every intention of the thoughts of his heart was only evil continually." Every intention . . . only evil . . . continually. Was the great flood able to wash that away?

Genesis 8:21 says, "The LORD said in His heart, 'I will never again curse the ground because of man, for the intention of man's heart is evil from his youth.' " No, each of us is contaminated from our conception with a sinful nature that makes every intention of our thoughts only evil continually. David described this inborn sinful nature in Psalm 51:5: "Behold, I was brought forth in iniquity, and in sin did my mother conceive me."

God's solution was a different washing, the water of Baptism, which is combined with God's word of promise and tied to the suffering, death, and resurrection of Jesus Christ, our Lord.

 CLEAR THE CONFUSION

Could the ark hold all the animal species?

Appearances can be deceiving, as the saying goes, and it certainly applies when we discuss Noah's ark. God has provided us with the measurements for the ark in Genesis 6:15, but we often gloss over this crucial detail because cubits have long since fallen out of use for measurement. In imperial units, a cubit typically measures around 18 inches, roughly the length from your elbow to your longest fingertip. Using this conversion factor, we can read the ark's dimensions as about 450 feet long, 75 feet wide, and 45 feet high. The volume of a ship this size would be immense—about 1.3 to 1.5 million cubic feet—and would have no trouble carrying only a pair of the landlocked, air-breathing animals that would not otherwise be able to survive the flood. Moreover, God sent Noah the creatures He sought to preserve according to their kinds, not species. In short, a kind of animal is a broader categorization than a species, which means that many fewer animals would have been necessary than we often imagine. Finally, modern depictions of Noah's ark often pack the ship with fully grown, adult animals, but nothing in the Scriptures indicates that this was the case. In fact, it would make more practical sense for God to have sent Noah juveniles or generally younger members of each kind to bring on the voyage. Animals in their younger years require less food, take up less space, are easier to care for, and have the very important reproductive capability and remaining life span necessary to repopulate the earth after the flood had subsided. All told, the author of Hebrews gives us the best approach to how we should read the account of the flood: "By faith Noah, being warned by God concerning events as yet unseen, in reverent fear constructed an ark for the saving of his household. By this he condemned the world and became an heir of the righteousness that comes by faith" (Hebrews 11:7). Noah built the ark and survived the journey by faith in God, trusting in God to take care of the things he couldn't see from his human perspective. As inheritors of that faith, we ought to take a cue from Noah and likewise trust that God provides for His people and creation.

WAYPOINT

What does this text show us?
After so much preparation, Noah and his family load the animals God had brought to them in the ark, and God closes them in. The rains fall from the heavens forty days and forty nights and the fountains of the great deep burst forth. The water covers the entire earth for 150 days before it begins to recede.

What does this text reveal about God's plan of salvation?
Though still early on in the Bible, here we glimpse a picture of God's final judgment. All those who do not believe in God's promises—that is the entire world minus Noah and his family—die. This is the ultimate end of all who do not believe in Christ. There will be a time when reality as we know it is over, when those who die apart from faith will join all those who have gone before to eternal separation from God forever in hell. God, however, saves Noah, his family, and a representation of the animals of the earth. Though the fallen creation does not deserve saving, because of God's pledge to one day save it through the Promised One, Jesus, God preserves believing Noah and his family.

What does this text uncover about our identity and calling as God's people today?
We live in a fallen reality that constantly rails against God's promises. Satan, the world, and our sinful flesh, however, cannot change what God has done for us in Jesus. Even greater than Noah's day, there will be a day when all things will pass away. Until then, God saves us and preserves us in His Christian Church. In fact, many church buildings over the centuries have been designed with nautical terms and structures in mind. In addition, the waters of the flood are a precursor to the waters of Baptism. By our Baptism into Christ, who suffered the punishment of sin and death we deserve, we are saved from the final judgment (see 1 Peter 3:18–22).

What details from this narrative reveal the scope of the devastation of the flood?

In what ways do you see both God's justice and God's mercy on display in the flood narrative?

How does knowing that the final judgment when Christ returns will be like the flood change how you live in and look at the world today?

PICTURE OF THE SAVIOR

Noah

For many people, having patience for something they want can be a grueling task. Noah's steady patience in his journey with God's plan for the flood was a precursor to the unyielding patience of Christ we experience in the Gospels. When God first revealed His incredibly specific design for the ark, Noah set about his duty with no complaining, no whining, and no back talk. He simply worked to build and prepare the ark—and work he did, for many long years before the task was finished. But his patience with God didn't stop there. Not only was Noah patient during the raging flood itself and the ensuing aftermath, but he also remained steadfast during the search for dry land, when both the raven and the dove came back with nothing at first. He waited inside the ark for a year and eleven days in all, confident in God's command over a situation in which he himself had zero control. Thousands of years later, Jesus would remain patient with His Father's timing for His ministry on earth, never moving or revealing Himself until the timing was just as God ordained. Though His disciples and the people around Him failed to understand the parables and sermons He would preach, Jesus stayed patient in love and continued to teach them repeatedly. And just as God shut Noah into the ark in order that he and his family might come out into a renewed world, so, too, did Jesus descend into a sealed tomb to rise again, having conquered sin, death, and the devil for us all.

From the text, consider what kind of person Noah was. What can we learn from Noah about who God is and how we are to live under Him?

 VISUALIZE

CLEAR THE CONFUSION

Where did all the water come from?

There are a few things to keep in mind when considering the gargantuan nature of the flood. When God first made the heavens and the earth, the great deep covered the entire earth until God made the dry land appear on the third day. The flood account might give us an idea where God put all that water in order to let the dry ground appear. Genesis 7:11 tells us God called water from below the earth ("the fountains of the great deep burst forth") and the skies ("the windows of the heavens were opened") in combination with the surface water of seas, lakes, and rivers to cover the landmasses. In His awesome might and command of His creation, surely God could move these waters across the land in ways we can hardly fathom or understand.

THE FLOOD SUBSIDES (8:1–19)

The waters recede and God sends Noah, his family, and the animals out of the ark to repopulate the earth.

 CLEAR THE CONFUSION

How long was the flood (40 days, 150 days, or 1 year and 11 days)?

Though it might seem contradictory that Moses recorded three different lengths of time in his discussion of the flood, his designations noted different stages of the larger event. The "forty days" referenced in 7:17 indicates the time when God brought the waters from the heavens and the great deep to cover the earth. The "150 days" mentioned in 7:24 describes the time the waters covered the earth before receding. This was a time of violent purging of evil, including every man and animal not aboard the ark, from the earth's surface by means of the fountains of the deep. Lastly, Moses totaled the entire length of time from when Noah boarded the ark to when he stepped on dry land once again at one year and eleven days.

What does the visual of the rainbow show us about God?

GOD'S COVENANT WITH NOAH (8:20–9:17)

Noah offers a sacrifice of thanksgiving, and God promises never to curse the ground despite mankind's evil nature still remaining. God establishes His covenant never to destroy the earth by another great flood. He uses the rainbow as a visual reminder of His promise. The sign of the rainbow is a visual of God hanging up or putting away His bow (used for archery).

NOAH'S DESCENDANTS (9:18–29)

Noah gets drunk and his son Ham dishonors and mocks him, while Shem and Japheth honor him. Noah places a curse on Ham's son Canaan and dies at the age of 950 years.

What does this tragic narrative reveal to us about living in this sinful world?

NATIONS DESCENDED FROM NOAH (10:1–32)

Genesis traces the nations that arose from Noah's three sons. These nations are to repopulate the earth.

VISUALIZE

The Genealogy of Noah

What details about this family tree stick out to you? Why? Is there something new you've learned by looking over this diagram?

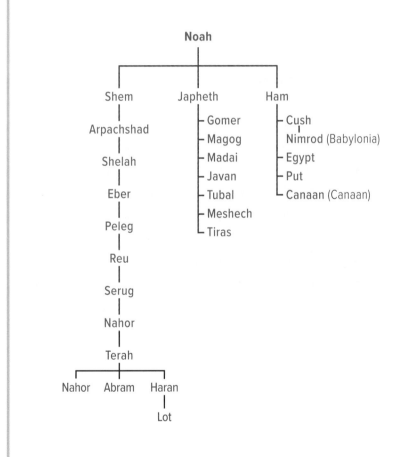

The Tower of Babel (11:1–9)

In what ways is this narrative similar to and different from the narrative of the flood just a few chapters earlier?

WAYPOINT

What does this text show us?

The narrative takes a brief turn toward a group of Noah's descendants. They refuse God's command to spread out and replenish the earth, as God had instructed immediately after the flood. Instead, they pool their resources and build a tower in defiance of God's command. God confuses their language so they can't understand one another, forcing them to spread out around the earth.

What does this text reveal about God's plan of salvation?

Though He saved believing Noah and his family from the flood, God still knows that the intentions of the hearts of humanity will be sinful from birth. Noah's descendants still follow the sinful pattern of thinking from before the flood. They think they know better than God, rebelling against His laws and authority. The building of the tower might have indicated that the people thought they could make a structure so tall that if God sent another flood, they would survive. It might also have been built in defiance of God, with the builders believing they could reach God. God's response comes not from feeling threatened that humans could do anything with a unified language but instead from knowing that the wickedness of their defiance of God and His rules would know no bounds if they did not spread out. Whereas the people foolishly think they can reach God, God instead intervenes in creation to preserve His people from complete self-destruction. God comes down to man, interacting with creation, to ensure that His plan of salvation will come to fulfillment one day in Christ.

What does this text uncover about our identity and calling as God's people today?

We now live in a diverse world, filled with many cultures and languages, all a direct result of what God did at Babel so long ago. After Jesus' ascension, at Pentecost, God gives His disciples the power to preach in the languages of the earth. The mission is clear for the Christian Church. We are to preach the Good News of Christ to all peoples, nations, cultures, and languages so that those who are scattered throughout creation may receive the gift of forgiveness and eternal life.

 CLEAR THE CONFUSION

Was God spiteful when He confused the people's language at Babel?

God wasn't spiteful when He confused the people's language at Babel. He foresaw the greater magnitude of sorrow and wickedness that the people would bring about (11:6) by rejecting His command for them to fill the earth (9:1) and by sticking together in one place to glorify themselves with a mighty tower (11:4). Out of His grace, God prevented them from working with one another in sin and dispersed them in order to carry out His plan of salvation through the hereditary line of Shem, Noah's son.

Why is pride, like the pride that the people of Babel demonstrated, such a destructive sin?

Why is it so important to remember that Christ's Church is worldwide? How can you continue to encourage Christians outside of your language, ethnic, or cultural group?

Imagine you were there when God confused the languages. From the text, what do you think you would have seen and experienced?

Babel → Pentecost (Genesis 11 → Acts 2)

Christ-centered gathering can produce much good. The events at Babel demonstrated what happens when the emphasis is on us and not on Jesus (which leads to bad, prideful things).

Even though the tower of Babel was an ugly example of humanity's rebellion against God and the evil that can result, it foreshadowed a much greater gathering of nations: Pentecost. While the people at Babel came together to glorify their own might, Peter quickly made it known that the phenomenon and blessing they were receiving in Jerusalem was from the Holy Spirit for the crowds gathered around the Gospel of Christ. The language miracle that occurred wasn't an undoing of God's work at Babel. After all, the people still spoke in their own tongues. The Holy Spirit allowed each one to hear the Good News about Jesus in his own language instead. This critical detail speaks volumes to the redemptive nature of Pentecost. While sin and rebellion against God can result only in division and discord, as it was for the people of Babel, it is only through the renewal found in Christ that far-flung nations can achieve true unity and come together under one banner once more.

SHEM'S DESCENDANTS (11:10–26)

Genesis traces the descendants of Noah's son Shem to Abram and his brothers. Of Noah's three sons, Shem continues the family line leading to the promised Savior.

The Book of the Patriarchs (11:27–36:43)

The second major division of the book of Genesis teaches us about the patriarchs (fathers), beginning with Abram and his descendants, whom God chooses to raise up a new nation from which the promised Savior will come. God will bless this nation to carry the promises and show God's holiness to the nations of the earth.

TERAH'S DESCENDANTS (11:27–32)

Genesis identifies the family of Terah, Abram's father. This list teaches us about Abram's wife, Sarai; his nephew Lot, who will travel with him to Canaan; and his brother Nahor, whose descendants will become wives for Abram's son Isaac and grandson Jacob.

Map of the Travels of Terah and Abram

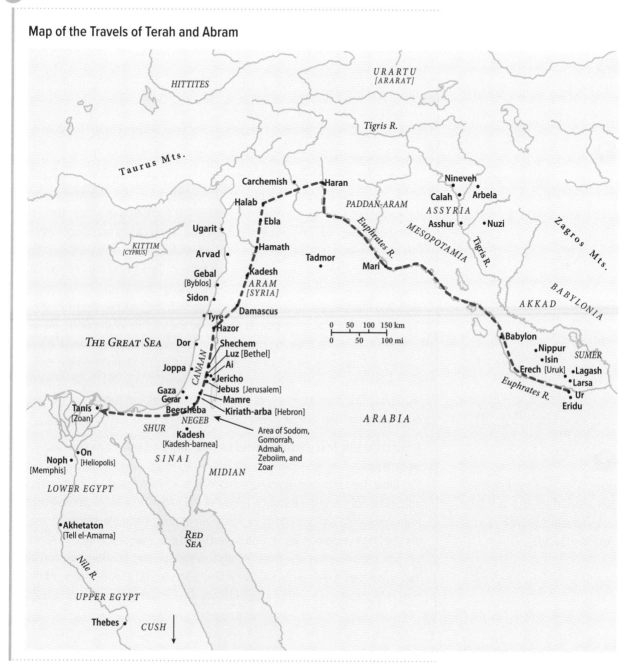

THE CALL OF ABRAM (12:1–9)

WAYPOINT

What details about Abram's travels stick out to you? Why?

How are all the promises that God gave to Abram fulfilled in their own ways in the rest of the Bible?

What does this text show us?
God calls Abram to leave his father's country and travel to a land to which God will guide him. He promises to make Abram's name great, raise a nation from him, and bless the world through his offspring, the promised Savior.

What does this text reveal about God's plan of salvation?
God chooses Abram from all the descendants of Noah and gives him a series of important blessings and promises. These promises help further narrow the scope and direction for the rest of the Bible. First, God promises that He will make Abram not only a father but also the father of a great nation with a promised land to inhabit. Second, God promises that Abram's name will be great, meaning he will be renowned and famous. Third, God offers a special promise that Abram will receive special blessings and favors in the world, including that those who oppose Abram and his family will be cursed. Finally, God offers an epic promise that, in Abram, all the families of the world will be blessed. This fourth blessing ties Abram into the promise God made in the Garden of Eden that an offspring of Eve would crush Satan and take away his power. This promise is fulfilled in Jesus, Abram's descendant, who some two thousand years later will die on the cross to defeat the powers of sin, death, and the devil for us.

How is our journey through life similar to and different from Abram's journey to the Promised Land?

What does this text uncover about our identity and calling as God's people today?
The Bible does not identify any specific reason why God chose Abram for this special role of being the founding father for the nation of Israel. God chose him from among the nations and gave him great promises and blessings. So, too, we are God's people today by God's mercy and grace alone, by faith in Jesus. We don't deserve the promises of forgiveness, life, and salvation offered by Jesus, yet they are ours. As we live in this fallen world, in anticipation of the new creation, we can rejoice in our identity as God's chosen people in Christ.

PICTURE OF THE SAVIOR

Abraham

Even though Abraham (Abram) failed to obey God perfectly throughout his life, his story still shines with a visual example of enduring faithfulness. God called Abraham out of idolatry to follow Him into a foreign land, promising that He would richly bless Abraham and his offspring. Abraham did so in the long run despite many complicating factors—infertility in old age, difficult travels into hostile nations, and even God's command to sacrifice the long-awaited son, Isaac, back to Him! Abraham truly believed in God, obeyed Him, and lived by the promise of God's grace, even when all things in his life seemed to contradict it. Yet his life is only a glimpse of such a faith. In the fulfillment of God's promise to which Abraham clung, Jesus would later embody this faithfulness perfectly by living a sinless life and obeying His Father in every way, even unto death on the cross for the salvation of mankind.

ABRAM AND SARAI IN EGYPT (12:10–20)

A famine drives Abram from Canaan to Egypt. Fearing he will be killed because of his beautiful wife, Sarai, Abram says she is his sister. Despite Abram's lack of faith, God protects Sarai's purity.

ABRAM AND LOT SEPARATE (13:1–18)

Under God's blessing, the flocks and herds of both Abram and his nephew Lot increase greatly. When the land can no longer support them all, Abram offers Lot his choice of directions to move. Lot chooses the better land of Sodom, which is known for its wickedness. God promises to give all the land to Abram's descendants.

What do the events of these narratives of Abram, Sarai, and Lot further reveal about who these people were and what they were like?

 **VISUALIZE**

The Land of Canaan

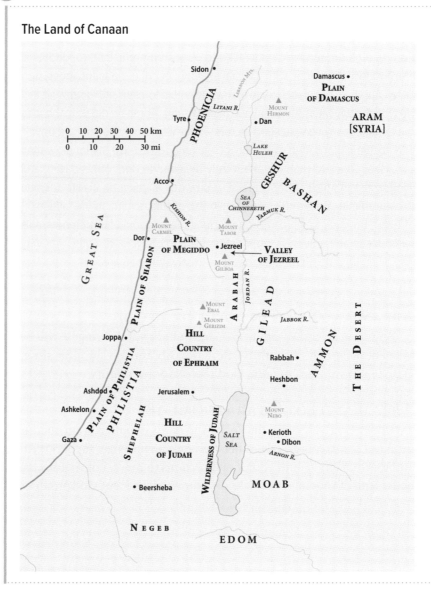

What does this further show us about Abram and the land he was living in?

ABRAM RESCUES LOT (14:1–16)

When rival kings defeat the kings of Sodom and its neighboring cities, Lot and his family are taken captive. Abram takes a small group of armed men, defeats the four powerful kings, and rescues Lot.

ABRAM BLESSED BY MELCHIZEDEK (14:17–24)

As Abram is returning after rescuing Lot, he is blessed by Melchizedek, priest of God. Abram gives him a tenth of everything.

LINK BETWEEN THE TESTAMENTS

Melchizedek → Jesus

Hebrews 7:1–3 has some interesting things to say about the mysterious prophet, priest, and king Melchizedek and his parallels with Jesus Christ:

> For this Melchizedek, king of Salem, priest of the Most High God, met Abraham returning from the slaughter of the kings and blessed him, and to him Abraham apportioned a tenth part of everything. He is first, by translation of his name, king of righteousness, and then he is also king of Salem, that is, king of peace. He is without father or mother or genealogy, having neither beginning of days nor end of life, but resembling the Son of God, he continues a priest forever.

What are some similarities and differences between Melchizedek and Jesus? In what ways is Jesus so much greater than Melchizedek?

God's Covenant with Abram (15:1–21)

As many years pass, Abram struggles to keep believing God's promise. God appears to Abram, renewing His promise of a son through whom He will build a great nation for Abram. Abram believes God, and God credits that faith to Abram as righteousness.

Many years after God had promised a child, the still barren Sarai takes matters into her own hands, giving her maid Hagar to Abram to father a son through her. Hagar treats Sarai with contempt when she conceives and flees when Sarai rebukes her. God promises to protect Hagar, who returns and gives birth to Abram's son Ishmael.

What do we learn about God's faithfulness despite our human weakness?

 CLEAR THE CONFUSION

Was God okay with husbands taking concubines, maidservants, or minor wives?

Concubinage, in which a man had sexual relations with other women who he did not marry in order to produce a suitable heir to his wealth when his wife was not able to do so, was one of many widely accepted legal practices of Abraham's and Jacob's day. Hagar was Sarai's Egyptian slave, and the laws Abram had grown up with permitted this behavior. While the Scriptures accurately report on these alternative means of childbearing, it does not advocate for them. In Abram's case, this surrogacy felt especially important because God had promised Abraham a son through which his descendants would be as populous as the stars in the sky (15:5). Sarai grew impatient with God and sought to bring about His will by her own hand. God did not intend this disobedient shortcut for Abram, and as a result, He set the descendants of Hagar's son, Ishmael, at odds with those of Isaac, whom Sarai would later bear by Abram.

Similarly, maidservants were a valuable gift the father of a bride could give to his daughter when she married. They could also serve as surrogate mothers, according to the recorded laws of the time period.

In Genesis 30, we will see Abram's grandson Jacob marry two sisters, Leah and Rachel. In a battle to win their husband's love, the sisters manipulate their maidservants Bilhah and Zilpah, twisting God's gift of marriage into something they could exploit in order to rear more children. God did not condone this for His people at any point, but even when they turned to these worldly practices, He still had mercy on them and included the twelve children born in His plan for the world's salvation through Christ.

What details from this narrative stick out to you? Why? What does this text reveal to you about who God is and how God works to fulfill His promises?

ABRAHAM AND THE COVENANT OF CIRCUMCISION (17:1–14)

Twenty-four years after first giving Abram the promise of a son, God appears again to Abram. He changes Abram's name to Abraham and makes a covenant of circumcision with him. Abraham and all his sons must be circumcised.

LINK BETWEEN THE TESTAMENTS

Circumcision → Baptism
(Genesis 17 → Matthew 3)

Circumcision was an outward mark that served to set Israel apart from all other people as the ones God had chosen to work through for His plan of salvation. Circumcision united them in a shared confession of faith that they belonged to God and remained within His lasting covenant promise. For thousands of years, Jewish boys would receive this sign just eight days after they were born so that they, too, might be brought into the faith and hope God gave to Abraham. Jesus, too, was circumcised eight days after His birth (Luke 2:21). Before Jesus began His earthly ministry, God established a new and similar practice through John the Baptist: Baptism. Jesus set His seal on this sacrament through His own Baptism and when He commanded Baptism in Matthew 28:19. Baptism would serve the same basic function—uniting believers by a visible sign—but for a renewed purpose. Paul's letter to the Romans helps us understand this best when he explains, "Do you not know that all of us who have been baptized into Christ Jesus were baptized into His death? We were buried therefore with Him by baptism into death, in order that, just as Christ was raised from the dead by the glory of the Father, we too might walk in newness of life" (Romans 6:3–4). Baptism not only links us with other

Christians in a common faith but also connects us directly to the promise of salvation found in the death and resurrection of Jesus Christ! The practice of circumcision, handed down from Abraham to generations of Jews, paved the way for Christ to establish one of the key sacraments that unites us in His salvation with believers across time.

Isaac's Birth Promised (17:15–18:21)

After commanding circumcision, God changes Sarai's name to Sarah and promises that Sarah will give birth to the son God had promised to Abraham. Abraham and Ishmael are circumcised in obedience to God's covenant. The preincarnate Christ and two angels visit Abraham and Sarah. The Lord promises that Sarah will give birth to Abraham's son by the same time next year. Sarah shows her skepticism by laughing at God's promise.

What do you think these name changes signify?

 VISUALIZE

Hospitality

In the ancient Near East, hospitality toward friends, family, and even complete strangers was a key part of the culture. Sharing a meal together indicated a close relationship between those gathered together. This was the case when the Lord appeared to Abraham and Sarah with two angels.

Abraham Intercedes for Sodom (18:22–33)

 WAYPOINT

What does this text show us?
After sending the two angels on to Sodom, the Lord tells Abraham the outcry against Sodom is great and He will destroy the city for its wickedness. Abraham thinks of his nephew Lot and begins bargaining, pleading with the Lord to spare the city for the sake of the righteous living there. God is pleased with Abraham's intercession and agrees to spare the city if ten believers can be found in it.

What can we learn about God's character from His interaction with Abraham?

Where do you see great wickedness in your community? How can you lovingly warn others tempted to sin to instead repent and receive forgiveness in Christ?

In what ways do you see both God's justice and God's mercy on display in this narrative?

As you read this section, envision what life in Sodom might have been like. What does this section reveal to you about God's judgment and His mercy?

What does this text reveal about God's plan of salvation?

The Lord Himself has come to talk with Abraham. This is usually interpreted as the preincarnate Christ. He sends two angels to personally witness the wickedness of Sodom and then destroy the inhabitants for their sins. God is a God of justice. There are consequences, both earthly and eternal, for humanity's disobedience against God's will. At the same time, God allows Abraham the opportunity to intercede, to bargain with Him over the minimum number of righteous people in the city that will move God to spare the city. We should not misinterpret this as Abraham holding up his righteousness against God's wrath. Instead, this interaction reveals God's patience and mercy, toward both Abraham and sinners. Though God is just, He is also merciful, not desiring that any should perish for their sins but that all would repent of their sins, believe His promises, and receive the gift of salvation (2 Peter 3:9). Though Sodom lacks ten believers and ends up being destroyed, God carefully spares the undeserving believers: Lot and his daughters. In Jesus, we see both God's justice and mercy in action. Jesus died on the cross to receive God's just judgment for the sins of the world, taking our place out of His mercy and love for us.

What does this text uncover about our identity and calling as God's people today?

This narrative serves as another picture of God's final judgment coming upon the wickedness of the world. The sins of Sodom and Gomorrah are reflected in the priorities and brokenness of this fallen creation. There will be a day when Jesus, the very one who sent the angels to proclaim God's judgment against Sodom, will return to judge the living and the dead. As God's people today, we are called not only to flee from the sinful temptations of the world but also to warn others to repent and receive forgiveness in Christ.

God Rescues Lot (19:1–22)

Two angels reach Sodom, and the men of Sodom try to molest them. The angels strike the men of Sodom with blindness and lead Lot, his wife, and their two daughters by the hand to flee the city.

God Destroys Sodom (19:23–29)

When the sun rises, God causes sulfur and fire to rain down on the city, totally destroying it. While they are fleeing, Lot's wife disobeys the angel's instructions and looks back. She is turned into a pillar of salt.

VISUALIZE

The Destruction of Sodom

God's angels led Lot and his family from the complete destruction of Sodom as burning sulfur rained down on the city.

LOT AND HIS DAUGHTERS (19:30–38)

Traumatized by the destruction of Sodom, Lot lives as a hermit in a cave with his two daughters. Seeing that their father will never provide husbands for them as he ought, his daughters get him drunk and sleep with him. In this way, Lot fathers a son by each of his daughters. Their descendants will form the nations of Moab and Ammon, which will usually live in hostility with the people of God.

ABRAHAM AND ABIMELECH (20:1–18)

While traveling through the southern region of Canaan, Abraham and Sarah spend time living in the Philistine city of Gerar. When Abraham says Sarah is his sister, the king, Abimelech, takes Sarah as a wife. God speaks to the king, warning him of death. Abimelech does not sleep with Sarah but restores her to Abraham and treats them well.

THE BIRTH OF ISAAC (21:1–7)

 WAYPOINT

What does this text show us?
When Abraham is one hundred years old and Sarah is ninety, the child of promise is finally born. Abraham and Sarah name him Isaac, roughly meaning "laughter," as a reminder of both how Sarah laughed at God at His original promise and how God gave them joy and laughter at Isaac's birth.

What does this text reveal about God's plan of salvation?
God gives Abraham so many great blessings during his life. The central promise is that the world will be blessed through Abraham's offspring, but for much of his life, it seems like God is not going to fulfill that promise. Without an heir, the promise of the Messiah made in the Garden of Eden

What details from this section further highlight the surprise and joy of Abraham and Sarah at the birth of their son?

How is the long-awaited birth of Isaac similar to and different from the long-awaited birth of the Messiah?

would have died off with Abraham. Yet God is faithful to His promises, even if they happen in unexpected ways. The promised line of the Messiah does continue through Isaac.

What does this text uncover about our identity and calling as God's people today?
God promises His people so many great things. He gives us forgiveness, life, and salvation. He promises that, in the end, all things will work together for the good of His people. He promises to hear our prayers. Yet, in the complexities of life, it sometimes feels like God's promises are far away or unrealized. From Abraham, and from so many others in the Bible, we see that God is faithful to fulfill His promises in His own way and His own time. We may not see how God works all things for our ultimate good or how He answers all prayers in His time, but we see from the Scriptures that He never abandons His promises. When Christ returns to make all things new, all of God's promises will be ultimately fulfilled for His people.

What else can you learn from this narrative about the nature of how God fulfills His promises?

GOD PROTECTS HAGAR AND ISHMAEL (21:8–21)

Abraham sends Sarah's maid Hagar and Hagar's son, Ishmael, away from Isaac. God protects them, and in time, Ishmael becomes the father of a great nation, the Ishmaelites.

A TREATY WITH ABIMELECH (21:22–34)

Abraham and the Philistine ruler, Abimelech, make a treaty, swearing not to deal falsely with each other or with the other's posterity.

THE SACRIFICE OF ISAAC (22:1–24)

 WAYPOINT

What does this text show us?
God commands Abraham to offer Isaac as a human sacrifice on a specific mountain. Abraham obeys, and right as he is about to slay Isaac, God stops him and provides a ram as a substitute sacrifice. This mountain becomes the site of the temple that King David's son Solomon will later build. The genealogy at the end of the chapter reminds us of the descendants of Abraham's brother back home. This is important because God will provide Isaac's future wife, Rebekah, from these descendants.

What does this text reveal about God's plan of salvation?
In this narrative, we see God testing Abraham's faith in His promise. In an even greater way, we see a clearer picture of God's plan of salvation. Abraham, the father, is commanded to kill his beloved son, yet is stopped and given

In what ways did Abraham and Isaac both remain faithful to obey God in the midst of commands they didn't understand?

What are some other connections you see between this narrative and Jesus sacrificing Himself for us on the cross?

a substitute sacrifice in a ram. On the cross, the Father does not spare His beloved Son, Jesus, but offers Him up as the sacrifice for all of us. In addition, it is the Angel of the Lord, the preincarnate Christ Himself, who stops Abraham from killing his son. In a dramatic and epic fashion, the Son of God prevents the end of the promised line of the Messiah, near the very place where, two thousand years later, He will give up His own life as the substitute sacrifice for the sins of the world.

What does this text uncover about our identity and calling as God's people today?

Though it would be tempting to read this narrative as an illustration of how God tests us, it is better to see this as a picture of God's mercy and grace. God made a promise to send the Messiah, and He maintained that promise even in the midst of things Abraham did not understand. As God's people today, we find great comfort in our identity as God's rescued people. Where we deserve nothing but death and eternal punishment for our sins, Jesus, the substitute sacrifice, has given His life in our place on the cross.

How has God remained faithful to you, showing His mercy and grace as you experience uncertainty and trials?

 ## PICTURE OF THE SAVIOR

The Ram (in the Sacrifice of Isaac)

During this climactic scene atop Mount Moriah, we get a sneak peek at the climax of God's great story of salvation. The sacrifice had been prepared: Isaac, bound on top of the altar, watched on as his father, Abraham, raised the knife according to God's command. Just as Abraham moved to draw the blade, however, God stopped him and sent a ram caught in a nearby thicket for him to sacrifice in his son's place. In the same way, God sent Jesus, the Paschal Lamb, to die on our behalf when we were ensnared by sin. He suffered our punishment. He bore the torment of sacrifice. Instead of you or me, He wore the crown of thorns in our place, just like the ram's head was caught in thorns so Abraham could sacrifice it to God in Isaac's place.

Why do you suppose there's so much detail in this text about the negotiation and purchase of this land? Why is this cave so important?

Sarah's Death and Burial (23:1–20)

Sarah dies and Abraham negotiates with the Canaanite people to purchase a burial place—a field with a cave in it and the only land Abraham will own in the Promised Land. It will be the site of the graves of Abraham and Sarah, Isaac and Rebekah, and Jacob and Leah.

 VISUALIZE

Field and Cave at Machpelah

Abraham purchased a field and the cave at Machpelah from Ephron the Hittite. This field and cave were located just east of Mamre (Hebron) in the land of Canaan.

When Abraham's wife Sarah died at age 127, he laid her body in the cave. Eventually, Isaac and Ishmael would bury Abraham there. Later, Isaac and his wife, Rebekah, would be buried there, then Jacob and Leah.

The entrance to the cave, now called the Cave of the Patriarchs, stands beneath a Muslim temple in Hebron.

Isaac and Rebekah (24:1–67)

 WAYPOINT

What does this text show us?
Abraham sends his servant back to his family in Ur to find and bring back a wife for Isaac. The Lord leads the servant to Rebekah, who agrees to return with him to be Isaac's wife even though she has never met Isaac. She returns with the servant and marries Isaac.

What does this text reveal about God's plan of salvation?
This narrative continues the central scriptural theme of the ancestry of the Messiah. This Promised One would come from the line of Abraham and Isaac. In the land of Canaan, there are no suitable women for Isaac to marry, and so Abraham's servant travels hundreds of miles back to Abraham's relatives to find a wife for Isaac. God provides Rebekah, who leaves her homeland, marries Isaac, and eventually bears sons, one of whom will continue the line of male heirs from which the Messiah will be born. As there was with Abraham, there is a lot of uncertainty over how the promised family line will move forward, but God provides Rebekah for Isaac, grafting her into the family tree of Jesus.

What does this text uncover about our identity and calling as God's people today?
This narrative highlights those who trust in God's promise and care even when the outcome is uncertain. The servant prays and trusts God will provide a wife for Isaac. Rebekah hears of God's promise to Abraham and Isaac, and in faith, she blindly follows the servant back to Canaan. In our daily lives of faith, we, too, are called to hear God's Word, pray, and trust His promises as we do the good works God has prepared for us to do.

What details in this narrative highlight the lives of both the servant and Rebekah's family back in Mesopotamia?

In what ways is Rebekah an unlikely character in the narrative of the Bible? What does her inclusion tell us about who God is and how He works?

What can we learn from the servant and Rebekah on how we are to fear, love, and trust in God above all things?

What sticks out to you or surprises you from this section about Abraham's life after Sarah's death?

In what ways do the blessings given to Abraham continue through the family line to Isaac?

What does the prophecy, and the controversy that surrounds it, show you about Isaac and Rebekah?

ABRAHAM'S DEATH AND HIS DESCENDANTS (25:1–18)

After Sarah dies, Abraham takes another wife and has six more sons. He gives each of them gifts, and he sends them away from his heir, Isaac. At the age of 175, Abraham dies. Isaac and Ishmael bury him with Sarah. A genealogy of Ishmael's descendants is also given.

VISUALIZE

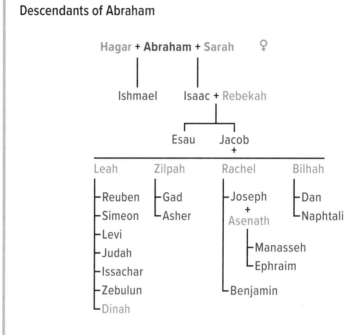

Descendants of Abraham

THE BIRTH OF ESAU AND JACOB (25:19–28)

After being barren for a time, Rebekah becomes pregnant with twins. The Lord reveals to Rebekah that the younger son will be greater than the oldest. Esau is born first, followed by Jacob. Rebekah favors Jacob, while Isaac favors Esau.

ESAU SELLS HIS BIRTHRIGHT (25:29–34)

Returning from the fields exhausted, Esau asks for some of Jacob's red stew. Jacob sells it to him for his birthright. The birthright gave the oldest son a double portion of the father's estate, and in this case, gave Esau the right to be in the line that led to the Christ. He despises that right, selling it to Jacob for a bowl of stew.

CLEAR THE CONFUSION

What is a birthright? Why is it such a big deal?

In Jacob's day, a birthright was a very important inheritance, typically passed from the patriarch of a given family to the eldest son. It contained a promise that the eldest son would gain leadership over the rest of the family and a greater share of his father's wealth when he died. Esau's willingness to trade away these esteemed privileges for a single bowl of stew showed his disrespect to his role in the family, and more significantly, his apathy toward God's promise of a Savior.

GOD'S PROMISE TO ISAAC (26:1–5)

A severe famine drives Isaac from the land where he is living as a stranger. God directs him to take his family to live among the Philistines rather than going down to Egypt. God promises to protect Isaac and extends to Isaac the promise He had given his father, Abraham, that the Savior will come from Isaac's descendants.

ISAAC AND ABIMELECH (26:6–35)

Isaac doubts God's promise of protection, and he lies to Abimelech. God protects Isaac and gives him prosperity and respect from the local rulers.

ISAAC BLESSES JACOB (27:1–46)

 WAYPOINT

What does this text show us?
Rebekah schemes with her deceitful son Jacob to steal the blessing Isaac intends to give Esau. While Esau is out hunting, Jacob and Rebekah disguise Jacob to resemble his older brother and lie to Isaac about his identity. Jacob receives the blessing God had promised, and when Esau returns and learns of the deception, he plots to murder Jacob.

What does this text reveal about God's plan of salvation?
For the first time, but not the last, in the family tree of the Messiah, there is controversy over who would be heir. The heir not only would inherit the lion's share of the inheritance possessions but also would receive the blessings of prosperity given first to Abraham. Isaac and Rebekah each favor one of their twin boys, and though Esau is the oldest, God has already prophesied to Rebekah that Jacob will be the greater of the two. Isaac despises God's choice by preparing to bless Esau. Rebekah distrusts God by taking matters into her

As you read this, consider all the careful steps that Rebekah and Jacob took to steal the blessing.

How are the words that Isaac spoke to Jacob similar to and different from the blessings God gave to Abraham in Genesis 12:1–9?

own hands to deceive her husband. In the midst of this dysfunctional family system of favoritism, deception, and hatred, God passes on the blessings to Jacob, who becomes the ancestor of the Messiah. But as we will see in the coming chapters, Jacob faces a difficult life. Despite the brokenness of this family, the promise of the Messiah is preserved and the narrative from now on will follow Jacob and his children.

What does this text uncover about our identity and calling as God's people today?

This narrative reveals the messiness of a particular family, as well as God's faithfulness to fulfill His will despite their infighting and sin. As God's people today, we cling to our identity as His children and are to check our own selfish pride and ambition. Instead of scheming, lying, and burning in anger over past sins, we are called to trust God's provision, repent, confess our sins to one another, and be reconciled in the name of Jesus.

How have you seen similar sins in your own life? How can you repent and work to be reconciled with others whom you have hurt?

Jacob Deceives Isaac

Though Isaac was blind by this time, he could still feel and smell. Jacob used the skins of animals so his skin would feel hairy like Esau's. And he wore Esau's clothing so he would have the outdoorsy smell of Esau. He was able to disguise himself as Esau and thus deceive his father.

How does God's promise to Jacob build upon what He promised to Abraham?

 CLEAR THE CONFUSION

What is a father's blessing? Why could Isaac give only one?

A father's blessing was equally as significant as the birthright. According to the custom of that time, a blessing was a rigid, binding pact made once and impossible to rescind. Isaac favored Esau and decided to commit all the blessings he could to his favored son and withhold them from Jacob. Once Rebekah and Jacob had tricked the blinded, elderly Isaac into committing the blessing to Jacob, that was it. There was no redoing or applying it twice. Even if it would have been possible for Isaac to give both brothers a blessing, Isaac had just committed all his blessings to Jacob, who he thought was Esau. So as a result, Jacob would rule over his brother, Esau. In other words, there was no way to give back some of the blessings to Esau after having committed them all to Jacob in such a total declaration.

Jacob Sent to Laban (28:1–5)

Learning of Esau's intent to murder Jacob, Rebekah convinces Isaac to send Jacob to her brother Laban to find a wife.

ESAU MARRIES AN ISHMAELITE (28:6–9)

When Esau learns his mother, Rebekah, is displeased with his Canaanite wife, he marries the daughter of Ishmael, Abraham's son by Sarah's servant Hagar.

JACOB'S DREAM (28:10–22)

 VISUALIZE

 WAYPOINT

What does this the text show us?
As Jacob flees from Esau, the Lord appears to him in a dream. He promises to be with him and passes on the promise that the Messiah will come from Jacob's family.

What details from this section stick out to you? What do they show about the nature of God's faithfulness to His people and promises?

How did Jacob respond to God's words and vision? How can we respond in similar ways as God's people today?

What does this text reveal about God's plan of salvation?
In a curious dream, God shows Jacob several things. First, God reiterates His blessings first given to Abraham. God also shows angels ascending and descending upon a ladder, with Him on top. This peek into the invisible world shows God's ongoing presence and interaction with creation. God does not abandon creation but intercedes in it. Jesus, Jacob's descendant, would recall this vision, stating that the angels ascend and descend on the Son of Man (John 1:51). The Lord, who was at the top of the ladder in Jacob's dream, descends into creation to redeem it. This is what Jesus came to do for us to fulfill the promises of the Messiah.

What does this text uncover about our identity and calling as God's people today?
In the busyness of life, it's easy to forget that God is working behind the scenes. He sends His holy angels to do His work. As the fallen powers of creation seek to tempt us to abandon our faith in Jesus, we know that God is constantly there. He who came to earth to redeem us will never leave us or forsake us.

Jacob Marries Leah and Rachel (29:1–30)

 WAYPOINT

What does this text show us?
Jacob travels to Abraham's homeland. There, he falls in love with his uncle Laban's younger daughter, Rachel. After Jacob works seven years to marry Rachel, Laban uses the darkness of night to deceptively give Jacob his older daughter, Leah, instead. In exchange for another seven years of work, Laban gives Rachel to be Jacob's wife.

What are some details that we learn about Jacob's character from this section?

What are all the ways in this section that God uses sinful people and broken relationships to carry forward His plan of salvation?

What does this text reveal about God's plan of salvation?
Jacob, who deceptively received the blessing from Isaac, is now deceived by his uncle. Using a cultural loophole as an excuse to enjoy the prosperity of Abraham's blessing passed from Isaac to Jacob, Laban passes off his older daughter as his younger daughter. Jacob ends up married to two sisters and works for his uncle fourteen years as a payment. From the beginning of this marriage, the seeds of animosity and discontent that he experienced with his own parents and brother are now passed on to his own family. Yet God still advances His plan of salvation despite this dysfunctional situation. Whereas Abraham had only one son with Sarah, and Isaac and Rebekah had two sons, through his marriages to Leah and Rachel, Jacob will have many sons. Though they will have their own enhanced dysfunction, the promise

that God made to Abraham, that he would be the father of a mighty nation, will begin to take shape in Jacob's family.

What does this text uncover about our identity and calling as God's people today?

Jacob's lies to his father and theft of his brother's inheritance were followed by his own uncle lying to him and robbing him of his first choice of a wife. Sins have consequences in this world. Though Jesus has forgiven us of our sins in eternity, God's will is that we act according to His commands here on earth. We are to flee from sins and avoid the devastation that comes with them. We are called to love and serve our neighbor, not take advantage of them (to often disastrous effect) as did Jacob and Laban.

What are some ways that we are tempted to take advantage of others? What can you do to avoid falling into those temptations?

 VISUALIZE

Jacob's Travels

The map below indicates the locations where Jacob traveled. Note the names of the cities as Jacob knew them and the names used later in time.

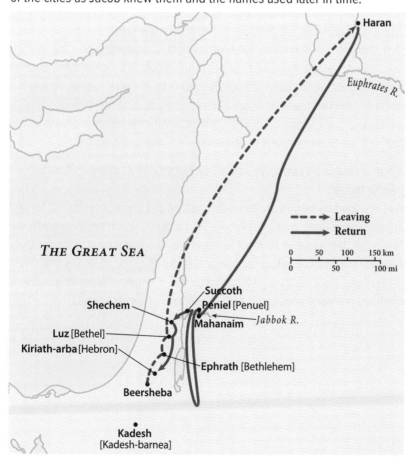

Jacob's Children (29:31–30:24)

Jacob resents and hates Leah because of her father's deception, but he loves Rachel. God has mercy on Leah, giving her the first four of Jacob's twelve sons, while Rachel remains barren. Leah's fourth son is Judah, whose descendants will include King David and Jesus Christ, the promised Savior.

WAYPOINT

What does this text show us?
Unable to have children of her own, Rachel gives Jacob her maidservant, Bilhah, who bears his fifth and sixth sons. Unwilling to lose ground to her sister, Leah gives Jacob her maidservant, Zilpah, who gives Jacob his seventh and eighth sons. Leah then gives Jacob his ninth and tenth sons and a daughter named Dinah. Finally, God remembers Rachel, and she bears Jacob his eleventh son, Joseph.

What does this text reveal about God's plan of salvation?
In a tragic series of events, the dysfunction of the family of Abraham, beginning with the favoritism shown to Jacob and Esau by their parents and extending through Laban's deception of Jacob, now continues with Jacob's wives and their surrogate maidservants. Yet, from the fight for power and prestige through childbearing, a cultural priority of the time, Jacob has eleven sons. Each of these sons will be the head of a full-fledged tribe of God's people, setting the political and geographical distinctions of God's people for centuries. Jesus, the Messiah, would come from the tribe of Judah, the fourth son, who would carry on the blessing given to Abraham.

What does this text uncover about our identity and calling as God's people today?
God designed marriage to be between one man and one woman for life. Though at times in the Bible, men marry more than one wife at a time, a cultural issue of the day, things never turn out favorably for those involved in these family situations. God desires that we honor the lifelong, monogamous institution of marriage, not use or abuse it for our own selfish gain. This calling to honor marriage is clearly contrasted with the turmoil in Jacob's family.

What details in this section highlight the specific pain and sorrow experienced by Jacob's wives and their maidservants in this dysfunctional race to bear sons?

Look over the names of the sons born to Jacob and consider which names are more familiar to you and which aren't. Where and when have you seen them before?

How can the Christian Church best uphold and support the lifelong, monogamous institution of marriage in our congregations amid so much dysfunction in the world around us?

VISUALIZE

After Rachel gave birth to a second son, Jacob was the father of twelve sons. The descendants of these twelve sons became the twelve tribes of Israel.

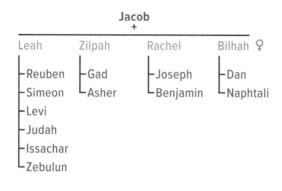

JACOB'S PROSPERITY (30:25–43)

After benefiting from the blessings God showered upon Jacob for fourteen years, Laban gives some of his flocks to Jacob for his continued labor. God blesses Jacob's flocks, and Laban's flocks shrink. So Laban changes Jacob's wages repeatedly, but God blesses Jacob, who prospers and becomes wealthy.

JACOB FLEES FROM LABAN (31:1–55)

Jacob's increasing wealth stirs greed and jealousy in Laban and his sons. After the Lord instructs Jacob to return to his home, Jacob flees without first telling Laban. Laban pursues and overtakes Jacob, but God warns him not to harm Jacob. The two make a treaty, and Jacob goes on with his family toward the Promised Land.

JACOB FEARS ESAU (32:1–21)

As Jacob draws near to Canaan, he fears that Esau still wants to kill him for what he had done so many years before. He brings his concerns to God in a prayer that repeats God's promises back to Him and is a wonderful model for our prayers. Then he makes careful preparations to soften his brother's anger when they reunite.

Jacob Wrestles with God (32:22–32)

 WAYPOINT

What details from this section further highlight both who Jacob is and how God works for His people?

What does this section reveal about God's patience and mercy toward us sinful creatures?

How can you build good daily habits that help you remember who you are in Christ and how He calls you to love and serve your neighbor?

What details unfold for you in this section that expand your understanding of Esau?

What does this text show us?

The whole night before he is to meet his brother, Jacob wrestles a mysterious man, God in human form. After refusing to let go of the man until he gets a blessing, Jacob receives a new name, Israel, meaning that he strives with God and man and prevails.

What does this text reveal about God's plan of salvation?

Jacob's entire story to this point has been one steeped in brokenness, deception, and running away. Before meeting with his brother for the first time in many years, Jacob fears that Esau will seek to kill him. The preincarnate Christ wrestles with him that night, preparing him for the uncertainty of meeting Esau the following day. This striving through the night reminds us of our Lord Jesus wrestling in prayer with His Father in the Garden of Gethsemane the night before He went to the cross. In the end, Jacob the deceiver is given a new name and a lingering ailment by the Lord to remind him of his struggle. Jacob is now Israel, not the deceiver but the one who strives in faith and wins. God has led Jacob through so much and has prepared him to now face his past with Esau. God does not let Jacob's weaknesses and insecurities hinder His plan of salvation, even intervening in physical form to wrestle with and form the character of Jacob.

What does this text uncover about our identity and calling as God's people today?

The Scriptures make it clear that our Christian identity does not mean that we will live without fear or struggle. Our sins are washed away in eternity by Christ, and our eternal future is assured by the cross of Christ. Even so, our old nature persists. As we wrestle against our own weaknesses and sinful inclinations, however, we can trust that God continues to form our faith and life. Our struggle to follow God's commands should drive us back to receive His Word and Sacraments, where God nourishes our faith and strengthens us for the tasks ahead.

Jacob Meets Esau (33:1–20)

Israel then goes out to meet his brother, Esau, who—surprisingly, after all this time—embraces and accepts him and his family. Both families live together peacefully in Canaan, and Israel buys some land near Shechem in which to settle.

THE DEFILING OF DINAH (34:1–31)

Shechem, a son of a prince of the land, rapes Dinah, Jacob's daughter by Leah. Shechem's father then proposes marriage between Dinah and Shechem, uniting the peoples. Israel's sons, outraged, deceptively agree to the marriage only if Shechem and the males of his people first get circumcised, to which they agree. While the men are recovering from circumcision, Dinah's brothers Simeon and Levi massacre all the men out of revenge and plunder their city.

GOD BLESSES AND RENAMES JACOB (35:1–15)

God commands Jacob's family to travel to Bethel. He protects them in their journeys from vengeful neighbors by instilling terror in the cities. Jacob tells his family to put away the false gods they had gathered. God appears again, confirms the new name He had previously given Jacob, and reestablishes His covenant with Israel, who builds an altar.

THE DEATHS OF RACHEL AND ISAAC (35:16–29)

As they journey from Bethel, Rachel goes into labor. After giving birth to her son Benjamin, she dies and is buried in what would be Bethlehem. The family travels to Mamre, where Isaac dies and is buried with Abraham and Sarah by his sons, Esau and Israel.

ESAU'S DESCENDANTS (36:1–43)

Genesis then turns from the main narrative to trace the family line and lineage of Esau. His many descendants form the nation of Edom, which neighbors the land of Canaan. Though Esau and Israel live in peace, their descendants will be fierce rivals in coming generations.

The Book of Joseph (37:1–50:26)

The final chapters of Genesis tell the story of the family of Abraham moving from the Promised Land to Egypt. It centers around Jacob's eleventh son, the firstborn of his favorite wife, Rachel.

Compare and contrast this tragic narrative surrounding Dinah with other accounts of Jacob's family. How do the children continue in the ways of their father?

VISUALIZE

Joseph's Dreams

Already Israel's favorite son, Joseph bragged about his dreams, increasing his brothers' jealousy.

JOSEPH'S DREAMS (37:1–11)

When Joseph, Israel's oldest son by Rachel, is seventeen, he gives a bad report to his father about his brothers. Joseph is already the favorite son, who is given a special cloak, and God gives Joseph special dreams. In these dreams, his brothers and father bow to him, and his brothers hate him even more for gloating about these dreams.

JOSEPH SOLD BY HIS BROTHERS (37:12–36)

 **WAYPOINT**

What do the conversations among the brothers and then between the brothers and their father reveal about Joseph's brothers?

In what other ways does Joseph's experience parallel or foreshadow Jesus' great act of salvation centuries later?

What does this text show us?
Joseph's brothers hatch a plan to get rid of him. They trap him and, after some debate on whether to kill him, sell him to slavers descended from Abraham's son Ishmael, who take him to Egypt. They trick their father, Israel, into thinking Joseph was killed by a wild animal.

What does this text reveal about God's plan of salvation?
Once more, the dysfunction of the family of Abraham spills over into greater sin. This time, the stakes are raised as Joseph's brothers plot to kill him. They throw him into a pit, fake his death, and in the end, sell him to slavers. Once again, however, God brings good out of the terrible acts and intentions of His chosen people in order to fulfill His purposes. Though nobody knows it yet, Joseph's time in Egypt will lead to the salvation of God's people. Joseph's experience here foreshadows Jesus' greater act. Joseph is thrown into a pit

and sold into slavery to preserve God's people. Jesus will be thrown into the pit of death to redeem God's people from slavery to sin.

What does this text uncover about our identity and calling as God's people today?

The family dysfunction in Abraham's descendants only seems to spiral further and further into greater sins from generation to generation. In fact, when the promised Savior comes, the children of Israel will demand His death at the hands of the Roman governor Pontius Pilate.

In Joseph's day, God will, in the end, use these experiences to reconcile the family. And in Jesus' day, He will use this hatred to reconcile Himself to all believers. But though God brings good out of this hatred, it does not mean that these familial patterns of sin and brokenness are good. Look to your own family. Where are there patterns of sin or dysfunction that continue from generation to generation? Know that God calls us to love and serve our neighbor, and in doing so, we can work to break unhealthy sinful patterns of behavior.

What is one sinful habit that you have continued from previous generations that you can seek God's help to break in your life right now?

👁 VISUALIZE

Joseph's Travels to Egypt

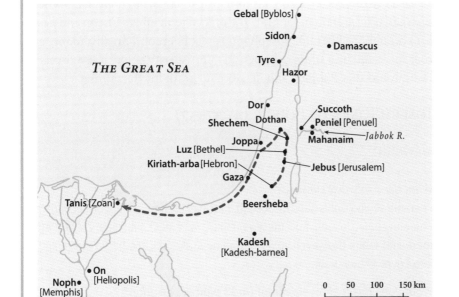

What does this section reveal to you about God's faithfulness to fulfill His promises despite the brokenness and sin of His people?

What does this section reveal about Joseph's character? What can we learn from his example in seeking to follow God's ways in uncertain or unexpected circumstances?

Judah and Tamar (38:1–30)

While Joseph is in slavery, his older brother Judah's two oldest sons are killed by God for their wickedness. Tamar, Judah's daughter-in-law, being denied a new husband by Judah, tricks Judah into sleeping with her and has a son by him. Thus, the line of the Messiah is preserved through Judah despite Judah's sins.

Joseph and Potiphar's wife (39:1–23)

Meanwhile, Joseph, in slavery, rises through the ranks to a position of authority over the house of his master, Potiphar. Potiphar's wife attempts to seduce Joseph, who refuses, and she falsely accuses him of attempted rape. Joseph is sent to prison and is eventually put in charge of all the prisoners.

Joseph Interprets Two Prisoners' Dreams (40:1–23)

In prison, Joseph meets two disgraced former officers of Pharaoh and interprets their dreams. The dreams of both come true. One officer is elevated back to his position but forgets about Joseph.

Joseph Interprets Pharaoh's Dreams (41:1–36)

After two years, Pharaoh has troubling dreams, but none of his wise men can interpret them for him. The official remembers Joseph and has him brought to Pharaoh. Joseph interprets Pharaoh's dreams to mean that there will be a seven-year period of prosperity before a seven-year famine and that Pharaoh should store up grain for the famine.

Joseph Rises to Power (41:37–57)

⊙ WAYPOINT

What does this text show us?
Pharaoh, seeing God's hand on Joseph, puts him in charge of Egypt, second to Pharaoh alone. Joseph, now thirty years old, oversees seven years of storing food, and when the seven years of famine strike, people begin streaming into Egypt to buy grain.

What does this text reveal about God's plan of salvation?
Joseph has been a slave for many years. Throughout that time, as far as the text tells us, God gives no indication of what He is doing. Even so, in his lowly estate, Joseph remains faithful to God. Here, through His miraculous hand, God raises Joseph up from slavery to sitting at Pharaoh's right hand, ruling the Egyptian Empire. Through this, God will not only save many thousands

In what ways did God turn Joseph's life around? How does Joseph's new life contrast to his previous life?

What do the names of Joseph's two sons (41:51–52) indicate about how God worked in and through Joseph to advance His great plan of salvation?

of people from starvation but also preserve Jacob and his family, including the line of Judah, which will lead to the Christ.

What does this text uncover about our identity and calling as God's people today?
Regardless of our stations in life, God calls us to be faithful to Him in our thoughts, words, and deeds. Though we fail and sin, He is always faithful and just to forgive us for the sake of Christ. Like Joseph, we do not know what will happen in the future, but we can cling to our identities in Christ, receive the gifts of His Word, and seek to love and serve our neighbor. It is unlikely that we will have a similar exalted status on earth like Joseph, but we who are in Christ will all receive a glorious exalted future in the new creation when Christ returns. Until then, we strive to remain faithful to God and do His will in our lives.

What is one way you can more intentionally love and serve your neighbor in your daily work?

JOSEPH'S BROTHERS GO TO EGYPT (42:1–38)

Jacob (Israel) hears there is food in Egypt and sends his sons, except Rachel's other son, Benjamin, to buy grain. They approach Joseph; he recognizes them, but they do not recognize him. To test their hearts, Joseph accuses them of being spies. He takes Simeon captive until his other brothers return with Benjamin.

JOSEPH'S BROTHERS RETURN TO EGYPT (43:1–34)

After their grain runs out in Canaan, Judah finally convinces Jacob to agree to send Benjamin with the other brothers back to Egypt. Upon arrival, Joseph receives them graciously, feeds them, reunites them with Simeon, and privately weeps upon seeing that his full brother, Benjamin, is alive.

JOSEPH TESTS HIS BROTHERS (44:1–34)

Joseph plants his cup in Benjamin's food sack and sends the brothers back to Israel. He then has them intercepted and tests them by accusing them of stealing. When the cup is found in Benjamin's sack, Joseph can test if the brothers will sacrifice Benjamin to save themselves. The brothers then plead with Joseph, concluding that God must be punishing them for their sin against Joseph. Finally, Judah offers himself in place of Benjamin.

Much of this portion of the book of Genesis is dedicated to laying out the details of how Joseph tests his brothers. What does this reveal to you about Joseph, his family, and his concerns?

JOSEPH PROVIDES FOR HIS BROTHERS AND FAMILY (45:1–28)

Joseph, overcome with emotion, reveals himself to his brothers. They are shocked that their brother is alive and in such a position of power, but Joseph assures them that this was God's plan. Pharaoh hears about this and commands Joseph's brothers to go and bring Jacob and the family to Egypt to live there. Jacob, upon receiving the report, is amazed and agrees to go.

 PICTURE OF THE SAVIOR

Joseph

As we near the end of our investigation of the book of Genesis, we see how Joseph illustrated Jesus' great mercy for all mankind when he forgave his brothers after all they had done to make his life miserable. Remember, Joseph's brothers did truly awful things to him. They mocked his prophetic dreams, planned to throw him in a pit, tore up his colorful robe from his father, and sold him into slavery, where he was destined for a life of misery. Only by God's grace did he rise in Potiphar's house and grow to be a prominent leader in Egypt. After much family drama, including a test, a reunion, and a time of prosperity for Joseph and his family, his father, Jacob, died. When this happened, Joseph's brothers were terrified that he would seek revenge on them for all the terrible things they had done to him in their youth. Instead of seeking the harshest punishment for them, Joseph had mercy on them and forgave them for their wrongdoings.

Notice these amazing parallels between Joseph and Jesus: Both were plotted against, seized by their own people, imprisoned, and handed over to foreigners. Joseph was put in a prison; Jesus was put on trial and condemned to death on a cross. Joseph was released from prison and set at Pharaoh's right hand to rule Egypt and save the people of many nations and his own family; Jesus arose from the dead, is seated at the right hand of God the Father, and rules all creation for the benefit of people of every nation and His own family of believers, the Christian Church.

About one third of Genesis is dedicated to telling the life of Joseph. What is Joseph's role in Genesis, and what does it reveal about God's great plan of salvation?

JOSEPH BRINGS HIS FAMILY TO EGYPT (46:1–27)

Israel makes a sacrifice, and God says He will make Israel a great nation in Egypt before returning His people to the Promised Land. Moses records the specific people who travel to Egypt.

JACOB AND JOSEPH REUNITED (46:28–34)

Joseph and Israel meet, embrace each other, and weep. Joseph plans to get his family settled in the land of Goshen, a proper part of Egypt for shepherds to dwell.

Jacob's Family Settles in Goshen (47:1–12)

 WAYPOINT

What does this text show us?
Joseph presents his father, Jacob, to Pharaoh, who agrees to settle Joseph's family in the ripe land of Goshen and provide whatever they need. Jacob blesses Pharaoh.

What does this text reveal about God's plan of salvation?
In a broad sense, this narrative helps set the context for the rest of the books of Moses. God's people are relocated from being nomads in the land of Canaan to settling in a fertile land amid the mighty power of Egypt. The book of Exodus explains that over the centuries, the Israelites' status changes from favored friends to slaves in Egypt, and the next four books of the Bible chart the course of the people from slavery in Egypt back to the land of Canaan. In a narrow sense, this narrative continues to show the power of God's promise directly to the descendants of Abraham. God blesses Joseph with the ability to interpret dreams, and ancient Jacob's supernatural blessings are so visible that the king of Egypt welcomes the blessing of Jacob in his midst. God is at work preserving and blessing His people, as well as setting up the next chapters of His plan of salvation in Egypt.

What does this text uncover about our identity and calling as God's people today?
It is easy to want to direct and chart our own course in life: where we want to live, what we want to do, and how we want to spend our years. This narrative reminds us that there are so many factors at work in the world that may derail our plans. Joseph's whole life was a series of changes and adjustments, setting aside his plans to faithfully serve those around him in various circumstances. But through it all, God was firmly in control. When major changes happen in life, it's most certainly unclear what will happen next. Frankly, God does not reveal His specific reasons to us. As we undergo transitions in location and livelihood, we can still seek to fulfill our calling to love and serve our neighbor, knowing and trusting that God is guiding everything in His creation for our good.

 What does this text show us about Joseph's relationship with Pharaoh, Joseph's relationship with Jacob, and Jacob's relationship with Pharaoh?

 How are the blessings that God gave to Abraham in Genesis 12:1–7 being further fulfilled in this narrative?

 What is a major life transition that you've undertaken? What new opportunities to love and serve your neighbor emerged as a result of that transition?

Joseph and the Famine (47:13–31)

The book of Genesis records how Joseph uses the famine to consolidate power over the whole land of Egypt for Pharaoh, creating a kind of sharecropping system. Jacob dwells in Egypt for seventeen more years, until he is age 147, and gathers his family to him as he prepares to die.

Jacob Blesses Ephraim and Manasseh (48:1–22)

Israel then adopts Joseph's sons, Ephraim and Manasseh, as his own and blesses Joseph. Joseph is displeased that Israel favors the younger Ephraim over the older Manasseh, but Israel insists that Ephraim will be the greater tribe. Moving forward, Joseph will receive the double inheritance of his father, as the tribes of Ephraim and Manasseh will each receive territory among the twelve tribes in Israel (since the tribe of Levi will have no land allotted to them).

What details, words, or phrases from Jacob's blessings stick out to you? Why?

Jacob Blesses His Sons (49:1–27)

Jacob blesses and prophesies over his other sons. Reuben, Simeon, and Levi, the oldest sons, receive particularly negative prophecies because of their sins, while Israel prophesies of Judah that royalty will come from his tribe. The Messiah will descend from the line of Judah.

Jacob's Death and Burial (49:28–50:14)

Finally, Israel commands his sons to bury him with Abraham, Sarah, Isaac, Rebekah, and Leah back in the cave Abraham bought in Canaan. Israel dies. Joseph mourns his father and has him embalmed. All of Egypt weeps for him seventy days. Joseph then slowly processes with his family and the officials of Pharaoh, including chariots and horsemen, to the cave of Machpelah to bury his father. They all then return to Egypt.

How is this interaction between Joseph and his brothers a microcosm of God's overall epic plan of salvation?

God's Good Purposes (50:15–21)

With Jacob dead, Joseph's brothers now fear retribution for what they did to Joseph and beg him for mercy and forgiveness. Joseph weeps, then shows them how God took what they once meant for evil and turned it to good by putting Joseph in the position to preserve His people and His promises. Joseph continues to provide for his brothers and their families.

The Death of Joseph (50:22–26)

Before Joseph dies at the age of 110, he prophesies that God will one day bring His people back to the Promised Land and makes his brothers swear that they will one day bury his bones there.

EXODUS

Welcome to Exodus

Exodus, literally "a going out," continues the account of the promises God gave to His people in Genesis. The descendants of Jacob find themselves slaves in the nation that once welcomed them. Subjected to cruel treatment and forced labor, they wait for the Lord's deliverance. Despite this treatment, Jacob's descendants have grown in number and strength.

Following years of forced labor and slavery, they are rescued when God appoints the unlikeliest of leaders to guide His chosen ones out from under the hand of Pharaoh. God's chosen people go out from the land of Egypt to the land promised to their forefathers.

As they journey through the wilderness, God provides for all their needs. He gives them His Law to guide their lives. He establishes their place and form of worship. As they travel, they face many challenges, yet their God never leaves them on their own. Instead, He cares for them and works through them to ultimately send His Son as the Savior of all mankind. Jesus rescued us from Satan and hell through His death and resurrection, and now He leads us through this sinful world to our home with Him.

You are about to read about Moses, the ten plagues, the Passover, and the crossing of the Red Sea. What narratives or images come to your mind when you reflect on this book? What are some specific things you'd like to learn more about?

Exodus at a Glance

- **Start:** Exodus begins about three hundred years after the death of Joseph, which is recorded at the end of Genesis.

- **End:** Exodus concludes with the completion and dedication of the tabernacle at Mount Sinai.

- **Theme:** God rescues His people from slavery in Egypt, and the Israelites begin their journey to the land promised to Abraham.

- **Author and Date:** Moses the prophet wrote Exodus in approximately 1446 BC.

- **Places Visited:** Egypt, the Red Sea, Mount Sinai/Horeb, and the wilderness in various locations

- **Journey Time:** The forty chapters of Exodus can be read in about three hours.

- **Outline:**
  - Israel Enslaved in Egypt (1:1–11:10)
  - Passover and Exodus (12:1–15:21)
  - Through the Wilderness to Mount Sinai (15:22–18:27)
  - Events at Mount Sinai (19:1–24:18)
  - Directions for the Tabernacle and Accessories (25:1–31:18)
  - Apostasy and Restoration (32:1–34:35)
  - Construction of the Tabernacle (35:1–40:38)

Five Top Sights and Spectacles of Exodus

The Ten Plagues (7:1–11:10) Follow along as God brings a series of plagues on the Egyptians in order to encourage Pharaoh to release the Israelites from their lives of slavery.

The Passover (12:1–51) Observe the preparations for the Passover meal as the blood of the lamb is applied to the doorway of each Hebrew home.

Crossing the Red Sea (13:17–15:21) Experience the drama as the Israelites find themselves caught between the Egyptian army and the waters of the Red Sea—until God performs a miraculous sign.

Manna, Quail, and Water (15:22–17:7) Watch as God, faced with starving and thirsty hordes, creates a daily source of food and provides water for His people.

The Ten Commandments (19:1–20:17) Learn the origin of the Law, which God has given to His people for all times.

Seeing Jesus in Exodus

Throughout the book of Exodus, Moses serves as prophet and high priest among the children of Israel. As prophet, Moses guides and leads the people from their life of slavery in Egypt as they head toward the Promised Land. As high priest, Moses offers sacrifices to forgive the sins of the people.

Jesus is our perfect Prophet and High Priest. He leads us from our slavery to sin into the promised land of the new heaven and new earth.

As our perfect High Priest, Jesus offers Himself as the complete and only sacrifice required for the forgiveness of our sins.

The blood of the Passover lamb spared the firstborn of the Hebrews from the angel of death. Jesus, our Passover Lamb, shed His own blood so we can be forgiven and have life eternal with Him.

Israel Enslaved in Egypt (1:1–11:10)

The first eleven chapters of Exodus explain how the descendants of Abraham, Isaac, and Jacob grow into a nation while living in Egypt, first free but then as slaves. God raises up Moses to lead them to freedom.

ISRAEL INCREASES GREATLY IN EGYPT (1:1–7)

The descendants of Jacob's twelve sons multiply rapidly in Egypt, growing exceedingly strong and filling the land.

 CLEAR THE CONFUSION

Hebrews and Israelites

Sometimes in the text, you will see God's Old Testament people described as *Israelites* (or *children of Israel*) and other times as *Hebrews*. The two terms are interchangeable and mean the same group of people. The term *children of Israel* may be used at times to specifically point to their heritage as descendants of Jacob (later called Israel).

PHARAOH OPPRESSES ISRAEL (1:8–22)

A new king unfamiliar with how Joseph saved Egypt comes to power. He fears the mighty number of Israelites and enslaves them. When they continue to grow in number, Pharaoh commands all baby boys of the Hebrews to be thrown into the Nile to drown.

Jacob's family increased from seventy people to possibly more than two million people. Why do you suppose they saw this huge increase?

THE BIRTH OF MOSES (2:1–10)

WAYPOINT

?

How did God ensure that Moses' mother continued to care for her son even after he was "adopted" by Pharaoh's daughter?

?

What other times does God use the sinful actions of mankind to carry out His plans?

?

What other Bible accounts can remind us of God's continuing care for His people?

What does this text show us?
A boy, descended from Jacob's son Levi, is born. To save her son from Pharaoh's death decree, his mother places him in a basket in the Nile River. Pharaoh's daughter names the Hebrew boy Moses and raises him as her own son.

What does this text reveal about God's plan of salvation?
God uses Pharaoh, who had decreed the death penalty on the Hebrew boys, to raise the boy who would one day save His people from slavery in Egypt. Despite the sinful, evil actions of mankind, God works to solve the problems of sin in this world.

What does this text uncover about our identity and calling as God's people today?
There are times when it is difficult to trust God's promises and live as His faithful people. But God is always with us, His promises are sure, and we can trust Him to care for us and bring us to Himself one day.

LINK BETWEEN THE TESTAMENTS

Moses → Jesus (Exodus 1–2 → Matthew 2)

Moses faced the threat of death as an infant when Pharaoh ordered all male Hebrew babies be tossed into the Nile. As a young child, Jesus faced a threat from Herod, who ordered the killing of all male babies born in Bethlehem. Jesus escaped this threat when Joseph moved his young family to Egypt, only returning once Herod had died.

MOSES FLEES TO MIDIAN (2:11–22)

Now a grown man, Moses kills an Egyptian who had beaten a Hebrew slave. When Pharaoh learns of the crime, Moses flees to Midian.

GOD HEARS ISRAEL'S GROANING (2:23–25)

The Hebrews probably felt as if God was ignoring them. How can we be reassured that God hears our prayers?

Forty years go by, but God hears the groaning of the Israelites, sees the Egyptian cruelty, and remembers His promise to Abraham to bring Israel out of Egypt to the Promised Land.

THE BURNING BUSH (3:1–22)

 WAYPOINT

What does this text show us?
While shepherding his father-in-law's flocks, Moses sees a bush burning on Mount Sinai. When Moses goes to investigate, God speaks to him from a bush that is on fire but is not consumed.

What does this text reveal about God's plan of salvation?
The people cry out to God to save them from the oppression of the Egyptians. In his encounter with the burning bush, Moses hears God's plan to use him to bring God's people out of captivity and into a land promised to Abraham. One day, God will send His own Son to rescue His people to bring them out of the slavery of sin and into our heavenly promised land.

What does this text uncover about our identity and calling as God's people today?
The Hebrews are God's chosen people, and He brings them out of slavery and into a land promised to the patriarchs. We are His chosen people who receive salvation through the death and resurrection of Jesus.

Moses marveled at a bush that burned without being consumed. What things in God's creation cause you to marvel?

God rescued His Old Testament people through the leadership of Moses. How did Moses set the stage for Jesus, our Savior from sin?

How does God remind us of our identity as His chosen people?

 LINK BETWEEN THE TESTAMENTS

I AM WHO I AM

When Moses asked God who he should say sent him to the Israelites, God revealed His personal name when He replied, "I AM WHO I AM. . . . Say 'I AM has sent me to you'" (3:14). In English Bibles, this special name of God is often identified with capitalized letters in the Old Testament.

In the Gospel of John, Jesus identifies Himself as "I am" more than twenty times. Additionally, Jesus uses a number of "I am" titles: I am the bread of life (John 6:22–59); I am the light of the world (John 8:12); I am the door (John 10:7–10); I am the Good Shepherd (John 10:11–18); I am the resurrection and the life (John 11:17–27).

Read through the text again. What significant moments do you see in this account?

MOSES GIVEN POWERFUL SIGNS (4:1–17)

Moses makes many excuses to avoid returning to Egypt. God gives him miraculous signs and provides his brother, Aaron, to speak for him.

MOSES RETURNS TO EGYPT (4:18–31)

Moses meets Aaron in the wilderness. They return to Egypt and show God's miracles to the elders of Israel, who believe and worship God. God has seen their affliction and has come to rescue them.

 CLEAR THE CONFUSION

Why did God seek to put Moses to death after sending him to Egypt?

God had commanded Abraham's descendants to circumcise their male children when they were eight days old. Moses had two sons by his Midianite wife, Zipporah, but had apparently circumcised only one of them. To save Moses' life, Zipporah went against her wishes and circumcised her other son. We know she was displeased, because she called Moses "a bridegroom of blood" (4:25). Now both of Moses' sons would be Hebrews (Israelites) instead of Midianites. God was satisfied and no longer sought Moses' death.

The people grumbled and accused Moses of making their lives worse. Why is it so easy to complain rather than thank God when things don't go the way we want?

Why did the people find it so difficult to trust God to do what He said He would do?

Why do you suppose Moses chose to include this genealogy here?

MAKING BRICKS WITHOUT STRAW (5:1–23)

Moses and Aaron tell Pharaoh God's command to let the Israelites go. Pharaoh refuses and punishes the Israelites by not providing straw for them to make bricks. The Hebrews grumble against Moses, accusing him of making things worse. Moses questions why God ever sent him.

GOD PROMISES DELIVERANCE (6:1–13)

Through Moses, God tells the Hebrews that He has seen their affliction and will bring them out of Egypt to the land He promised to Abraham, Isaac, and Jacob. Though the people don't believe Moses, God commands Moses and Aaron to speak to Pharaoh.

THE GENEALOGY OF MOSES AND AARON (6:14–30)

Moses establishes his authority as a descendant of Jacob's third son, Levi. Despite his genealogy, Moses doubts Pharaoh will listen to him.

MOSES AND AARON BEFORE PHARAOH (7:1–13)

The Lord sends Moses and Aaron to demand the Israelites' release but warns that Pharaoh will not listen. God threatens His judgments on Egypt to force the release of His people. Moses performs the first sign

God had given, but Pharaoh's wise men replicate the sign. Pharaoh's heart is hardened against God's warning.

THE FIRST PLAGUE: WATER TURNED TO BLOOD (7:14–25)

When Moses was born, Pharaoh ordered the Hebrew baby boys to be thrown into the Nile. Now in the first plague, God turns the Nile, and every pool of water in Egypt, to blood, killing the fish and filling Egypt with their stench. When the Egyptian magicians do the same, Pharaoh's heart remains hardened.

THE SECOND PLAGUE: FROGS (8:1–15)

God brings frogs up out of the Nile to fill the land of Egypt; however, the magicians also bring up frogs. Pharaoh asks Moses and Aaron to plead with God to remove the frogs. God strikes the frogs dead. But Pharaoh hardens his heart yet again.

The Nile was considered the source of life in Egypt. How does this fact make the first plague so significant?

Pharaoh asked Moses to bring an end to the plague. How did God respond despite Pharaoh's continued rejection?

💡 CLEAR THE CONFUSION

Were the plagues real miracles or naturally occurring events?

Each of the ten plagues described in Exodus was a miracle from God meant to humble the Egyptians for their idolatrous practices. As similar as they may have been to other natural events common in that time, their severity, their appearance in close succession, and their coinciding with God's Word as given through Moses and Aaron indicate that these were produced and sent by God. The plagues were meant to reveal God's complete superiority over the Egyptian gods and magicians. The specific nature of these plagues toppled the perceived might of the magicians' trickery; the gods' dominion over the weather, light, and darkness; and even Pharaoh's powerful lineage so that he would relent and allow the Israelites to leave their captivity in Egypt.

THE THIRD PLAGUE: GNATS (8:16–19)

Aaron strikes the ground with his staff, filling the land with gnats. When the Egyptian magicians cannot duplicate the miracle, they tell Pharaoh this is the finger of God. But just as God had warned, Pharaoh hardens his heart and refuses to listen to them.

THE FOURTH PLAGUE: FLIES (8:20–32)

God sends great swarms of flies throughout the land of Egypt but protects the Israelites from the plague. Pharaoh begs Moses to plead with God to remove the flies, promising the people could go to worship God. Despite God's mercy, Pharaoh hardens his heart again.

THE FIFTH PLAGUE: EGYPTIAN LIVESTOCK DIE (9:1–7)

Pharaoh's stubborn heart continues to destroy Egypt's economy. God slowly ratchets up the intensity of the plagues. This time, the plague kills all the Egyptian livestock without harming the Israelites' livestock. After this plague, God hardens Pharaoh's heart.

Despite the destruction in Egypt, God spared the Israelites. How does this show God's continued care for His people?

 CLEAR THE CONFUSION

Who hardened Pharaoh's heart?

God commanded Pharaoh to set Israel free. But during the first five plagues, Pharaoh hardened his own heart and refused to listen.

After that, God hardened Pharaoh's heart. That means the Holy Spirit stopped working to make him believe and obey God. Without the Holy Spirit's help, Pharaoh became so stubborn he didn't care when Egypt's animals died and all its crops were destroyed. He wasn't even afraid when God said his first son would die.

After that, Pharaoh finally let Israel go free. But even then, he changed his mind and sent his army to bring Israel back. The Egyptian army was destroyed at the Red Sea. Pharaoh could not blame God for this; he had disobeyed God's command many times.

Jesus called this the sin against the Holy Spirit (Matthew 12:31). People do this when they refuse to let the Holy Spirit help them feel sorry for their sins and look to Jesus to save them. When people do this enough, God may harden their hearts too.

The magicians suffered so greatly from boils that they could not stand. Consider a time when you suffered greatly. How did God respond to your suffering?

THE SIXTH PLAGUE: BOILS (9:8–12)

Painful sores break out on man and beast throughout Egypt. Covered with sores, the Egyptian magicians cannot stand before Moses. "The LORD hardened the heart of Pharaoh" (v. 12), giving him up to unbelief.

THE SEVENTH PLAGUE: HAIL (9:13–35)

God has been merciful to Pharaoh and the Egyptians, slowly increasing the severity of the plagues, giving Pharaoh a chance to obey and save his people and land. God shows His mercy once more, sending a plague that destroys half the harvest while sparing the remainder.

THE EIGHTH PLAGUE: LOCUSTS (10:1–20)

Pharaoh's stubborn heart causes God to harden it. In punishment, God sends a plague that destroys the remaining crops in Egypt's fields, yet none of Israel's crops are harmed.

THE NINTH PLAGUE: DARKNESS (10:21–29)

God strikes the Egyptians with three days and nights of darkness, showing God's power over the sun, which the Egyptians worshiped as a god.

A FINAL PLAGUE THREATENED (11:1–10)

After the plague of darkness, Pharaoh threatens Moses with death if he sees his face again. Moses promises he will not return, but only after threatening one final plague: the death of every firstborn son in Egypt—just as Pharaoh had commanded the death of every male Hebrew baby eighty years earlier.

Passover and Exodus (12:1–15:21)

God uses one final plague to free the Hebrews from slavery in Egypt. The Passover will be the most important event in the Old Testament, reminding God's people of His deliverance and pointing ahead to the promised Savior, who will be sacrificed to save the world from their sins.

THE PASSOVER (12:1–28)

WAYPOINT

What does this text show us?
God instructs Moses and Aaron in the preparations for the Passover. The Hebrews are to prepare the lamb and their household in advance of the final plague. The application of the lamb's blood to their doorways with the hyssop branch seals the promise of God's mercy toward His people.

What does this text reveal about God's plan of salvation?
Through the blood of the Passover lamb, the children of Israel are spared from the final plague of death. Through the blood of Jesus—the Lamb of God—we are spared from eternal death and separation from God.

Through this final plague, God brought an end to the oppression of His people in Egypt. How did God bring an end to our oppression under sin and death?

The blood on the doorpost sealed God's promise of salvation to the children of Israel. How has God sealed His promise of salvation to His people today?

What does this text uncover about our identity and calling as God's people today?
We are God's chosen people. Just as He kept His promise of protection and deliverance to His people in the time of Moses, He remains with His people today.

 PICTURE OF THE SAVIOR

The Passover Lamb

Nestled within God's institution of the Passover for the Israelites lies an image of Jesus that, ironically enough, often gets passed over next to the plagues and miracles of the exodus from Egypt. Nevertheless, the Passover lamb serves as a humbling sketch of Christ's work to come. According to God's command, the lamb must be one "without blemish, a male a year old," taken from the choice sheep and goats of the household (12:5). The Israelites were instructed to kill it at twilight of the fourteenth day of the first month and dab its blood on the two doorposts and lintel of their home, for only by this sign would God pass over the home and leave the firstborn child alive. Jesus would come as the Son of God, a man who lived without blemish or sin in His life. This was the one who was sacrificed upon the cross during the Jewish remembrance of that fateful night, and His precious blood was smeared on the beams of the cross in order that the curse of death because of our sins should pass over us too.

THE TENTH PLAGUE: DEATH OF THE FIRSTBORN (12:29–32)

At midnight, the Lord strikes down every firstborn male in every household of Egypt. Pharaoh calls Moses and Aaron and implores the Israelites to leave Egypt.

 LINK BETWEEN THE TESTAMENTS

Hyssop

The blood of the Passover lamb was applied to the doorposts using a hyssop branch. Among Jesus' words spoken on the cross was "I thirst" (John 19:28). The soldiers used a hyssop branch to hold the sponge filled with sour wine to quench His thirst.

The Exodus (12:33–42)

The Israelites prepare to leave Egypt so quickly they cannot leaven their bread. The Egyptians gladly hand over their silver and clothing as they urge the Israelites to leave. About 600,000 men (with an estimate of perhaps even two million people total) depart Egypt.

Institution of the Passover (12:43–51)

The Lord instructs the Israelites to remember the day of their release from slavery in Egypt. Honoring His instruction, God's people will celebrate the Passover meal every year, culminating in the Last Supper at the time of Jesus.

After years in slavery, the Hebrews finally experienced freedom. How did they respond to this newfound freedom?

LINK BETWEEN THE TESTAMENTS

Passover → The Lord's Supper (Exodus 12 → Matthew 26:17–29; Mark 14:12–25; Luke 22:7–23; 1 Corinthians 11:17–32)

In the Passover, we see how God gave the Israelites a meal to remember His grace when He orchestrated their escape from bondage in Egypt and how He had given them safety from the angel of death that came to kill the firstborn children of Egypt. The specific preparations and dishes were meant to remind them yearly of the trial and the recognition of God as He who meets all their needs. Similarly, Jesus instituted a new meal under a new covenant in which He reminds us of His sacrifice and, more importantly, offers the real presence of His body and blood for our spiritual nourishment each time we eat and drink in the Sacrament of the Altar.

The Feast of Unleavened Bread reminded the people of God's mercy. What other reminders of His mercy do we see?

Consecration of the Firstborn (13:1–2)

God had rescued each firstborn of the Israelites from the final plague; now He claims them as His own.

LINK BETWEEN THE TESTAMENTS

The Dedication of the Firstborn (Exodus 13:1–2 → Luke 2:22–38)

The Law required the dedication of the firstborn males to the Lord in response to the fact that God spared the firstborn of the Israelites. Firstborn sons would have been consecrated to serve God, but God consecrated the entire tribe of Levi to serve Him, including the priests. God included a provision by which parents could buy back, or "redeem," their firstborn sons from this service by sacrificing a lamb (13:13). Later, God also included a different option for redeeming a son from this service, a payment of five shekels of silver (Numbers 18:16).

The Gospel of Luke recounts the presentation and dedication of Jesus in the temple as Mary and Joseph's firstborn. He is the fulfilment of this theme in the Old Testament. Jesus is the sacrificial lamb, who paid His life to buy back humanity from sin, death, and hell. He is the firstborn from the dead.

The Feast of Unleavened Bread (13:3–16)

God instructs the people to celebrate an annual feast of unleavened bread for seven days following the celebration of the Passover. This feast serves as a reminder of God's work in helping His people escape slavery in Egypt. The firstborn must be redeemed through sacrifice.

Pillars of Cloud and Fire (13:17–22)

The Lord leads His people along the route He chooses by a pillar of cloud in the daytime and a pillar of fire at night.

Crossing the Red Sea (14:1–31)

WAYPOINT

Take a moment to really examine this narrative. What details stick out to you as you read this? Why do they stand out for you?

What other connections can you see between Moses' deliverance through the Red Sea and our deliverance to new life through Baptism?

What does this text show us?
When the Egyptians realize the loss of their labor force, Pharaoh orders the army to pursue the Israelites. Seeing Pharaoh's chariots approaching, the Israelites cry out to the Lord. The Lord instructs Moses to raise his staff and lead the people forward through the Red Sea on dry ground. As the Egyptian chariots pursue the Israelites into the sea, Moses raises his staff again and the sea closes over the army.

What does this text reveal about God's plan of salvation?
In this event, God displays His power to fulfill His promises and save His people from their enemies. God brings them through the chaotic uncertainty of the Red Sea and delivers them safely to the other side. Moses was appointed the prophet God would use to deliver His people from bondage, through danger, to the Promised Land. Through the cross and empty tomb, Jesus, the greater prophet that Moses prophesied would come after him (Deuteronomy 18:15), delivers us through the waters of Baptism to the eternal promised land of the new creation.

What does this text uncover about our identity and calling as God's people today?

We are surrounded by uncertainty and danger. In this event, a central component of the exodus narrative, God shows through miracles by His mighty hand that He keeps His promise to deliver His people. In Christ, God has been faithful to deliver us. Though we may be surrounded by uncertainties and dangers in this life, our entire hope rests in what Christ has done for us. No matter what happens in this world, He has a promised land awaiting His people.

How are Christians today like and unlike the Hebrews in this narrative?

 CLEAR THE CONFUSION

How did Pharaoh have horses to chase down the Israelites?

While the Scriptures say that "all the livestock of the Egyptians died" in the fifth plague (9:6), there are a few things to keep in mind as we read. First, Moses makes a clear distinction in his original proclamation that only the livestock in the field would be struck down by the plague. He said nothing about the horses Pharaoh kept in his personal or military service, so we are allowed to infer that these God left untouched. Moreover, none of the Israelite horses were killed in the plague either. Pharaoh could have taken their horses to counteract his own losses after God destroyed his equestrian forces. Lastly, we must note the hyperbolic use of the word *all*. Just as one might say that a brutal frost in spring destroys an entire fruit crop, the overwhelming majority was Moses' greatest concern when he wrote the account. Individual animals may have remained, but the fact of the matter is that the once substantial and powerful force was snuffed out. We often use this same literary device today and should grant Moses and the other biblical writers its use as well.

THE SONG OF MOSES (15:1–21)

Now safely across the sea, Moses sings a song of praise, recounting the work of the Lord to save His people from the Egyptian army.

Through the Wilderness to Mount Sinai (15:22–18:27)

God leads the Israelites to Mount Sinai, where He had earlier appeared to Moses in the burning bush. God will reveal Himself to His people there.

What specifically was the complaint of the people, and what can we learn about God from how He answered them?

Bitter Water Made Sweet (15:22–27)

When the only water source available tastes bitter, the Israelites show their impatient unbelief as they grumble against Moses. God instructs Moses to toss a log into the water, which miraculously makes it sweet.

 VISUALIZE

Journey through the Wilderness

This map shows a route the Israelites may have traveled as they journeyed from Egypt, across the Red Sea, and to Mount Sinai.

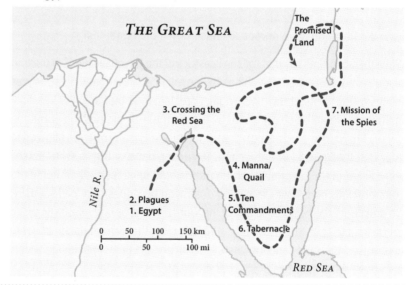

Bread from Heaven (16:1–36)

 WAYPOINT

In what ways is the manna symbolically significant to God's people in this section?

What does this text show us?

The people grumble against God, complaining about the lack of food in the wilderness. Moses goes to God, who promises to "rain bread from heaven" (v. 4). God listens to their grumbling and gives them one evening of quail that land on the ground and cover the camp. In the morning, the ground is also covered with dew that leaves a flakelike bread behind. God instructs the Israelites to gather just what they need of this bread (known as *manna*, or "what is it?") for each day. On the day before the Sabbath, they are to gather enough for two days, since they are not to labor on the Sabbath. The people will eat this manna (but not the quail, which God provides only one more time) for the next forty years as they wander in the wilderness.

What does this text reveal about God's plan of salvation?

As God leads the people through the wilderness, He provides for them despite their complaints. In fact, during the forty years of the wilderness, God exclusively and miraculously provides for all their daily needs: food, water, protection, and even clothing that never wears out! All the while, God uses this time to refine and discipline His people. Around 1,500 years later, Jesus says that He is the bread from heaven (John 6:32–35). Just as God provided daily manna for the people in the wilderness, Jesus, the bread of life, provides for all our spiritual needs as we journey to the new creation.

What does this text uncover about our identity and calling as God's people today?

Jesus is the bread of life that came from heaven. As we receive His gifts in Word and Sacrament, we are spiritually formed and strengthened. God also provides for our daily needs. In the Lord's Prayer, Jesus taught us to pray, "Give us this day our daily bread," which certainly points us back to this episode in the lives of God's people. Just as the people in the wilderness were to trust in God's care, we, too, are to thank God for all the good gifts He provides for us.

LINK BETWEEN THE TESTAMENTS

Manna from Heaven → Feeding of the Four Thousand/Five Thousand (Exodus 16 → Matthew 15:32–39; Mark 6:30–44; Luke 9:10–17; John 6:1–14)

Despite the faithlessness and grumbling of His people, God continued to provide for them as they journeyed through the Sinai wilderness. Even though God gave them all that they needed for physical nourishment in the form of manna, some of the Israelites sought to take more for themselves out of gluttonous and greedy desires. The Israelites discovered, however, that sustenance would come by God's hand alone and not their own machinations. We can see the same kind of providence in the New Testament when Jesus feeds a crowd of five thousand men (many likely with families) with only five loaves of bread and two fish. His disciples, whom He had tasked with attending to the crowd's needs, didn't believe it could be done and urged Him to send them away. Yet through Jesus, the meager amount of food became bountiful, feeding the crowd and even providing leftovers for the group. Across time, God continually shows us how He fully provides for His people in all their needs and teaches us to ask for the same: "Give us this day our daily bread."

Consider how God has provided for your spiritual and physical needs today. What are some things that you generally take for granted but can be especially thankful for today?

God provided for the people's needs each day. How does God assure us of His daily provision for our needs?

God provides all we need in this life and the next. Where do we pray for God to provide our "daily bread"?

Water from the Rock (17:1–7)

⊙ WAYPOINT

What details does God point out here in His command to Moses? How do you think these details work together to make a visual for the Israelites about God's deliverance?

How else is water used in the Bible to show God's work in His creation? Watch for this theme as you continue to read.

What does this text show us?

Once again, the people grumble about their thirst. They are so upset with Moses that they are on the verge of open rebellion. The Lord instructs Moses to strike a rock with his staff, and water gushes forth, satisfying the thirst of the people.

What does this text reveal about God's plan of salvation?

As God's people grumble against Him, God provides a powerful visual. He actually appears on a rock before them in the wilderness and has Moses strike the rock with his staff, and water flows from the rock. Later, the apostle Paul identifies this Rock as the preincarnate Christ, who provided spiritual sustenance for God's people in the wilderness (1 Corinthians 10:4). This is a great mystery, but it once again shows that the Second Person of the Trinity, who would one day be incarnate in human flesh, was with God's people throughout the Bible (usually identified as the Angel of the Lord). Just as God provided water for His people through Christ when Moses struck the rock in the wilderness, so, too, He provides forgiveness of our sins through Christ, our Savior, whose side was pierced on the cross.

What does this text uncover about our identity and calling as God's people today?

Water plays an important role in God's plan of salvation. Jesus' side was pierced on the cross, and out came blood and water. From ancient times, this has been connected with God's gifts of the Lord's Supper and Baptism. Through Baptism, we are connected to Christ's death and resurrection. God cared for His people in the wilderness through water from the rock; He provides for us today through His gifts given through Christ.

What are some other possible connections between how God provides for His people in this narrative and how He provides for us through Jesus?

👑 **PICTURE OF THE SAVIOR**

Water from the Rock in the Wilderness

Traveling through the desert can be quite thirsty work, and for the Israelites on their way to the Promised Land, this was no exception. Eventually, their complaints grew to such a degree that Moses cried out to God for help, fearing that he would be stoned by his own people. God sent him and the Israelites rescue in the form of a fountain of water that gushed from a rock in the wilderness. We often find ourselves in a spiritual wilderness of our own, groaning and complaining to God that He would quench our thirst. He has given us Jesus for exactly that purpose—for He is the one who was broken for us to unleash a never-ending stream of grace and forgiveness that leads to an eternity with Him. As He said to the woman at the well in John 4, "Whoever drinks of the water that I will give him will never be thirsty again. The water that I will give him will become in him a spring of water welling up to eternal life" (v. 14).

ISRAEL DEFEATS AMALEK (17:8–16)

As Moses holds his hands aloft, Joshua leads the Israelite army in battle against the nomadic Amalekite tribe. When Moses grows weary, Aaron and Hur help hold up Moses' arms until the army claims victory. God commands Joshua to remember and God Himself will not forget this unprovoked attack on His people. (See also 1 Samuel 15:1–3.)

JETHRO'S ADVICE (18:1–27)

Jethro, Moses' father-in-law, brings Moses' wife, Zipporah, and their two sons to join Moses in the wilderness. When Jethro observes how much time Moses spends dealing with issues between the Israelites, he suggests a system to help manage these situations.

Jethro guides Moses to set up a system of administration. How could your church structure help your pastor focus on Word and Sacrament ministry?

Events at Mount Sinai (19:1–24:18)

God reveals Himself to Israel on Mount Sinai. He proclaims His Ten Commandments to the nation, then gives Moses the Book of the Covenant.

ISRAEL AT MOUNT SINAI (19:1–25)

Once the Israelites arrive at Mount Sinai, the Lord calls Moses up to the mountain, with instructions and warnings for the people. The people consecrate themselves as they await the Lord's appearance on the mountain in smoke and the sound of the trumpet.

Why do you suppose God wanted the people to prepare themselves for His appearing?

👑 PICTURE OF THE SAVIOR

Mount Sinai

Mount Sinai was more than just a rest stop for the Israelites as they journeyed to the Promised Land. This important landmark foreshadowed the spectacular way Jesus came to redeem all who were separated from Him. At the foot of this mighty mountain, God came down and visited His people in order to quell doubts and draw up the covenant with Moses, the intermediary He had chosen. His coming was a spectacle; the Scriptures recount the thunder, lightning, fire, and smoke that accompanied His descent to Mount Sinai. Jesus revealed His presence in the world in much the same way—not by thunder or fire but by miraculous signs and wonders—so that He could establish a new covenant, one paid for by His blood and given for all who would believe in Him.

THE TEN COMMANDMENTS (20:1–21)

▶ WAYPOINT

What does this text show us?

God gives Moses the Law in what we call the Ten Commandments (the Bible labels them as the ten commandments, or words, in Exodus 34:28 and elsewhere, but without numbers). The Israelites wait in fear as the mountain is covered in smoke, as the trumpet and thunder sound, mixed with flashes of lightning.

What does this text reveal about God's plan of salvation?

Here, God gives His people the moral law, that is, God's expectations for how we should live as His human creatures. This applies to all people of all times. Note that these laws are different from God's ceremonial and civil laws in the Old Testament, which cover politics and worship practices and are no longer applied to God's people after Christ. God's moral law is absolute, and none apart from Christ can keep it perfectly. In Christ, we have the forgiveness of sins for when we fail to keep God's Law.

What details stand out to you that you may not have noticed before about this famous section of the Scriptures?

How do these commandments act like a mirror for us, showing us our sins and our need for a Savior?

What does this text uncover about our identity and calling as God's people today?

It's easy to overlook how this section both begins and ends. The first statement God makes to Moses is not a command but a reminder of what He has done for His people by delivering them. After God gives the commandments, and His people shrink in terror from His presence, God tells the people to not be afraid. The Christian life involves regular self-examination, confession, and absolution. As it was for God's people at Mount Sinai, however, life as God's people today is always bookended by God's faithfulness to keep His promises. Forgiven and loved in Christ, we strive to live God-pleasing lives in our thoughts, words, and actions.

How do the commands of God build off of one another? What does that show us about God's good design for His human creatures?

 LINK BETWEEN THE TESTAMENTS

The Ten Commandments → The Sermon on the Mount
(Exodus 20 → Matthew 5–7)

The Ten Commandments sealed the covenant God made with His people after guiding them from captivity in Egypt, but their importance didn't end there. God designed these moral imperatives as timeless markers of His character for all who believe in Him to honor and uphold. In the New Testament, Jesus returned to these basics in His Sermon on the Mount and shed light on the deeper truth embedded in each one. Over the course of His ministry, many schemers sought to trick Jesus by twisting the Commandments away from God's original intent, but He remained steadfast in the Word and repelled their efforts. Even after Jesus fulfilled the Law and ascended into heaven, the apostles and early church leaders dealt with issues that required a test by God's Law in order to resolve the situation. The Ten Commandments are still a reflection of God's desire for our lives as His people, but there is no more condemnation for those who believe in Christ.

LAWS ABOUT ALTARS (20:22–26)

During the time Moses spends on Mount Sinai, God provides laws beyond the Ten Commandments. In this section, God gives the people directions for building altars of sacrifice from earth or stone. He reminds the people not to make idols of silver or gold.

LAWS ABOUT SLAVES (21:1–32)

God provides detailed instructions for the treatment of slaves. Every seven years, all Israelite slaves were to be set free.

Laws About Restitution (21:33–22:15)

The Lord gives specific rules concerning liability when dealing with livestock, crops, and other possessions.

Laws About Social Justice (22:16–23:9)

God lays out detailed directions for dealing with relationships, personal property, and the needs of others.

Laws About the Sabbath and Festivals (23:10–19)

In six days, God created the heavens and the earth, then rested on the seventh day. Thus He establishes the pattern for worship on the Sabbath. Additionally, the Israelites were to celebrate three festivals each year: the Feast of Unleavened Bread, the Feast of Harvest, and the Feast of Ingathering.

Conquest of Canaan Promised (23:20–33)

God tells the people that an angel will lead them as they journey to the Promised Land. While they will have victory over any who oppose them, they must not worship the gods of their enemies.

The Covenant Confirmed (24:1–18)

Moses and the religious leaders of Israel meet with the Lord on the mountainside to renew God's covenant with the people. There, they eat and drink in God's presence, as we do in Holy Communion. Finally, Moses ascends into the cloud on the mountaintop, where he spends forty days and nights.

 LINK BETWEEN THE TESTAMENTS

The Number Forty

The number forty occurs many times throughout the Scriptures. In Genesis, rain fell for forty days and nights as God destroyed the sinful world while sparing Noah and his family. Here, God gives His Law as Moses spends forty days on Mount Sinai.

Just after His Baptism by John, Jesus faced forty days alone in the wilderness being tempted by Satan. The devil tempted Jesus to break the Law, which God the Father had given on Sinai.

Moses spent forty days receiving the Law from the hand of God. How does Moses' time spent with God emphasize the importance of the Law?

Directions for the Tabernacle and Accessories (25:1–31:18)

God gives Moses plans to build a portable worship space where He will be present with His people, traveling with them from Mount Sinai through the wilderness to the Promised Land.

 CLEAR THE CONFUSION

What was the tabernacle? Why was it so important?

The tabernacle was a large tent and extended worship area where God dwelled among His people. It was constructed meticulously from the finest materials to best reflect heaven on earth. In this place, which was set up at the heart of the Israelite encampment in each region they rested, the high priest interceded on behalf of the Israelites and offered sacrifices to God as a means of grace and forgiveness of sins. Because of the tabernacle, God was able to stay close to His people, guide them to the Promised Land through Moses, and provide for their needs as they traveled.

CONTRIBUTIONS FOR THE SANCTUARY (25:1–9)

As Moses prepares to build the tabernacle, the people have opportunity to contribute materials needed for the creation of the sanctuary.

THE ARK OF THE COVENANT (25:10–22)

The ark of the covenant will serve as the centerpiece for the sanctuary in the tabernacle. The Lord gives Moses detailed instructions for the design and construction of the ark.

The Israelites gave from their riches for the building of the tabernacle. How do we see this practice carried out today?

 VISUALIZE

Ark of the Covenant

The ark of the covenant was designed to serve as God's throne in the tabernacle. The ark held the stone tablets of the Ten Commandments, a container of manna, and Aaron's staff. The pure golden cover of the ark, known as the mercy seat, had replicas of two angels, one on each end. God spoke to Moses from between the two angels on the mercy seat.

The Table for Bread (25:23–30)

The golden table for bread in the sanctuary would hold special bread, named the bread of the Presence, reminding the people of God's presence with His people as they travel from place to place.

How can we share the message of God's grace in Christ with those in our family and community?

 PICTURE OF THE SAVIOR

Jesus the Living Bread

The table for the bread of the Presence in the tabernacle served to remind the people of God's presence and provision as they traveled through the wilderness and entered the Promised Land. In the New Testament, Jesus calls Himself our living bread: "I am the living bread that came down from heaven. If anyone eats of this bread, he will live forever. And the bread that I will give for the life of the world is My flesh" (John 6:51). Through His death and resurrection, our sins have been washed away and we have life through the living bread.

The Golden Lampstand (25:31–40)

The golden lampstand, covered with golden blossoms and other details, would give light to the interior of the sanctuary.

 LINK BETWEEN THE TESTAMENTS

Jesus, Our Light

The golden lampstand gave light to the tabernacle. God gives us His light. We see this theme of God as light repeated throughout the Scriptures. One of the most notable examples appears in John's Gospel, where he calls Jesus "the light [that] shines in the darkness" (1:5).

The Tabernacle (26:1–37)

Detailed directions for the fabric and leather coverings for the tabernacle explain the organized layout of this portable worship site. The Israelites will move this portable sanctuary with them throughout their travels.

◉ VISUALIZE

A Cubit

A common unit of measurement found throughout the Bible is the cubit. It was the distance between an adult's elbow and the tip of his longest finger.

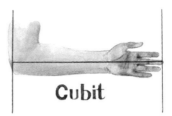

THE BRONZE ALTAR (27:1–8)

The bronze altar serves as the location for the burnt offerings made by the priests on behalf of the people. This altar was to be outside the tent but within the courtyard surrounding the tabernacle. Like all the tabernacle's fixtures, the altar is designed to be portable.

THE COURT OF THE TABERNACLE (27:9–19)

God instructs that the enclosed tent of meeting be surrounded by an open-air courtyard delineated by fabric walls.

◉ VISUALIZE

Court of the Tabernacle

The tabernacle would continue to serve as the center of worship in Israel until Solomon built the first temple in Jerusalem. The layout of the tabernacle, with the Holy Place and Most Holy Place surrounded by an outer courtyard, would be repeated in the design of the temple in Jerusalem.

Worshipers entered the space before the tabernacle through the courtyard. How did this entrance make an impact on worshipers?

OIL FOR THE LAMP (27:20–21)

No detail is overlooked in God's instructions for the tabernacle. Even the olive oil used to fuel the lamps in the tent of meeting is described.

THE PRIESTS' GARMENTS (28:1–43)

This chapter describes in fine detail the garments made specifically for the priests to wear while appearing before the Lord on behalf of Israel and while leading the people in worship. The breastplate of the high priest would contain twelve gemstones, one for each of the sons/tribes of Israel.

CONSECRATION OF THE PRIESTS (29:1–46)

God appoints Aaron and his sons as priests for the Israelites. To prepare these men for their duty as priests, God establishes sacrificial ceremonies to set them apart for His service. (Read more about this consecration in Leviticus 8.) These blood sacrifices point forward to Christ's sacrifice on the cross for our sins.

God appointed the Levites as the religious leaders for the children of Israel. How do we set apart men for service in the church today?

THE ALTAR OF INCENSE (30:1–10)

The altar of incense would be used daily for the burning of incense as a sacrifice to God. The smoke ascending to heaven reminds the people of their prayers ascending to heaven.

THE CENSUS TAX (30:11–16)

As the people report the number of their family members, they must pay a tax. Each family pays half a shekel.

THE BRONZE BASIN (30:17–21)

Aaron and the priests need to wash their hands and feet before entering the tent of meeting or making offerings to the Lord. The basin for washing stands between the bronze altar and the tent of meeting.

THE ANOINTING OIL AND INCENSE (30:22–38)

The Lord gives Moses the recipes for mixing the incense and anointing oil used in the tabernacle. God specifies to use only the finest ingredients and to reserve the use of these for His house alone.

God wants our finest. How did the people give of their best?

OHOLIAB AND BEZALEL (31:1–11)

Moses appoints Oholiab and Bezalel as the two artisans to lead the production of the special fixtures for the tabernacle. God declares He has filled Bezalel with the Holy Spirit and appointed Oholiab, and He uses their talents to serve the whole nation.

THE SABBATH (31:12–18)

Once again, God reminds the people to regularly celebrate the Sabbath. As this chapter closes, God gives Moses the two stone tablets of the Law written by the Lord Himself.

 CLEAR THE CONFUSION

Does God grow tired or weary?

God's nature is plainly described throughout the Scriptures. He is almighty, everlasting, unchanging, and spirit, not able to grow exhausted or fatigued (Isaiah 40:28; John 4:24). The Hebrew word *shabat*, from which we derive *Sabbath*, has the primary meaning "to cease" or "to stop." When Moses writes that God rested (shabat), he uses it in that primary sense and does not attribute the human quality of tiredness to God's character. This is an example of anthropomorphism, or the literary device in which human qualities are given to nonhuman entities. The Holy Spirit often inspires writers to use this tool throughout the Old Testament to best explain elements of God's character to us in understandable ways.

Apostasy and Restoration (32:1–34:35)

During Moses' time receiving instructions from God on the mountain, Israel constructs and worships a golden calf idol, but Moses intercedes for the people and God restores His covenant with Israel.

THE GOLDEN CALF (32:1–35)

 WAYPOINT

What does this text show us?
The people grow impatient waiting for Moses to return from Sinai, so they convince Aaron to create a golden idol. The consequence for their behavior is swift and severe when Moses returns. After grinding the idol into a powder, he forces the people to drink the remains. The Levites arm themselves with swords and strike down three thousand men who led the rebellion. Moses returns to the mountain, and God directs him to follow the angel to the place the Lord would have them go.

 What kinds of consequences do we face for our sins?

What does this text reveal about God's plan of salvation?

Moses returns to the Lord as he pleads for God's mercy on the people despite their blatant sin. In a greater way, our Savior, Jesus, pleads with our heavenly Father to forgive our sins for His sake. Through His death and resurrection, the price of our sins has been paid.

What does this text uncover about our identity and calling as God's people today?

We are a sinful and broken people, and we live with constant reminders of our brokenness. The sinful idols of this world, including unhealthy pleasure, power, and wealth, are constantly tempting us to ignore God's Law and serve ourselves. Yet through Christ, we have been made right with God. In response to the grace given us, we can instead serve one another.

How can we respond to the assurance of salvation won for us through the work of Jesus Christ?

 VISUALIZE

The Golden Calf

Idols used during the time of the Old Testament typically took the form of animals; some idols combined human and animal features. Idols could be small pocket-size household gods or large statues used for public ceremonies. The Scriptures don't tell us how big the golden calf Aaron made actually was, but it would have been large enough for Moses to see from a distance as he descended Mount Sinai.

 CLEAR THE CONFUSION

Sometimes we, like Aaron, have ridiculous excuses for our sin: "I threw it [gold] into the fire, and out came this calf" (v. 24). How should we respond when confronted with our sin?

Why didn't God kill Aaron when he formed the golden calf?

God spared Aaron's life after he formed the golden calf because Moses interceded on his—and the rest of Israel's—behalf. Moses trusted in God's promise to Abraham, Isaac, and Jacob and asked for His mercy on account of His faithfulness. Aaron was an important part of preparing Israel in God's greater plan for humanity's salvation in the early days of the priesthood. This doesn't mean he got off the hook; Aaron and the entire nation suffered harsh consequences due to their idolatry. God sent a plague upon the Israelites and threatened to withhold His blessings for the rest of their journey to the Promised Land. Moses called the Levites to purge their own circles of idolatrous kin and rededicate themselves to God before they could be charged with priestly duties. Aaron may not have suffered death, but God surely punished him and Israel for turning away from Him.

THE COMMAND TO LEAVE SINAI (33:1–6)

The people mourn, removing their jewelry as God forces them to leave Mount Horeb (Sinai). Despite their stiff-necked, stubborn behavior, God reminds them of His promise to give them a land of their own.

THE TENT OF MEETING (33:7–11)

At each encampment, Moses erects the tent of meeting outside the camp. The Lord would descend in a pillar of cloud to speak with Moses. This tent of meeting would be used by Moses before the tabernacle was constructed.

MOSES' INTERCESSION (33:12–23)

Moses pleads for the Lord to show him His glory. God warns that no one can see His face and live so He hides Moses in a cleft of the rock and passes by so that Moses only sees His back.

How can we listen for God's direction and guidance in our lives?

 PICTURE OF THE SAVIOR

Moses

At the climax of Exodus, Moses looks remarkably like Jesus in his willing sacrifice for the people of Israel, whom he loved greatly. While Moses was atop Mount Sinai receiving the Ten Commandments from God, the Israelite people had turned their backs on God and began worshiping a calf made of gold, instead, at the behest of Aaron. Upon his return, Moses found the Israelites in the middle of this pagan worship, just as God told him they would be, and sought to help them escape from their sin. He went back up Mount Sinai to plead with God that He might spare His people, offering his own removal from the Book of Life in exchange for theirs. In this way, Moses commits himself to the same atoning exchange that Jesus would carry out on the cross at the end of His life. While God rejects Moses' offer, since the sacrifice of one sinful man cannot pay for the deeds of another, Moses foreshadowed Christ's complete and acceptable sacrifice, taking the sins of all upon Himself in order that we are counted righteous before God.

MOSES MAKES NEW TABLETS (34:1–9)

Moses returns to Sinai with two new stone tablets that he has chiseled out of rock to replace the first set, which he destroyed upon seeing the golden calf. God reminds His people of the consequences of their sin while at the same time reassuring them of His compassion and forgiveness.

THE COVENANT RENEWED (34:10–28)

As Moses concludes his time on Mount Sinai, the Lord reaffirms His covenant with His chosen people. The requirements for participation in festivals and the promise to drive out their enemies from the Promised Land are reaffirmed.

THE SHINING FACE OF MOSES (34:29–35)

When Moses descends from Mount Sinai, his face glows from his encounter with the Lord. The people gather to hear the Word of the Lord from Moses.

Construction of the Tabernacle (35:1–40:38)

SABBATH REGULATIONS (35:1–3)

God commands that the Sabbath will be celebrated on the seventh day as a day of rest.

CONTRIBUTIONS FOR THE TABERNACLE (35:4–29)

Moses appeals for the materials and craftsmen needed to construct the tabernacle. The people may have responded with such great generosity out of thanksgiving for the fact that God did not destroy them for their idolatry.

CONSTRUCTION OF THE TABERNACLE (35:30–36:38)

Moses' face glows from his encounter with the Lord. When will we experience the full glory of the Lord?

Why do you think that, when Moses made an appeal for material goods and time, the people responded as they did?

Review the sections concerning the construction of the various elements of the tabernacle. Consider how these elements all fit together.

⊘ WAYPOINT

What does this text show us?
Bezalel and Oholiab guide the craftsmen in the construction of the tabernacle according to the directions God gave to Moses. These chapters record the details concerning the fabric panels that make up the tabernacle.

What does this text reveal about God's plan of salvation?
God establishes the tabernacle as His dwelling place, where He comes to His people. In addition, the tabernacle serves as the place where the people offer the sacrifices for their sins. Jesus, our human tabernacle, came to dwell with His people in human form. Through His death and resurrection, we receive forgiveness and salvation.

What does this text uncover about our identity and calling as God's people today?
We live as God's chosen people; He desires to be with us in all aspects of our lives. We also use the gifts and talents that God has given us to love and serve our neighbor, just like God used Bezalel's and Oholiab's talents.

MAKING THE ARK (37:1–9)
Moses records the details of the actual construction of the ark of the covenant.

MAKING THE TABLE (37:10–16)
Moses then records the detailed construction for the table of the bread of the Presence.

MAKING THE LAMPSTAND (37:17–24)
An explanation of how the craftsmen form the golden lampstand, which gives light to the tabernacle, follows.

MAKING THE ALTAR OF INCENSE (37:25–29)
God's directions for the construction of the altar of incense are completed by the craftsmen. The smoke of the incense rising to heaven represents the prayers of the faithful ascending to heaven.

MAKING THE ALTAR OF BURNT OFFERING (38:1–7)
The bronze altar used for the burnt sacrifices is constructed according to God's direction.

MAKING THE BRONZE BASIN (38:8)
The bronze basin, used by the priests for cleansing, is completed by the craftsmen.

MAKING THE COURT (38:9–20)
The craftsmen complete the panels, which like the fabric panels used to form the tent of meeting form the courtyard surrounding the tent.

The Lord directs the final building of the tabernacle. How might the craftsmen have responded to seeing their work come together?

These sections describe the construction of various elements of the tabernacle. Compare these historical fixtures to churches today.

EXODUS

MATERIALS FOR THE TABERNACLE (38:21–31)

Moses gives an accounting of the costly precious metals used in the construction of the tabernacle.

MAKING THE PRIESTLY GARMENTS (39:1–43)

The weavers and artisans use the boldly colored yarns to create the garments for Aaron and his sons. The golden breastplate, set with precious and semiprecious stones, represents the twelve tribes of Israel.

 VISUALIZE

The Priestly Garments

The artisans used the directions given in Exodus 39 to complete the special garments for the high priest. Each of the twelve precious and semiprecious stones set into the priest's breastplate represents one of the tribes of Israel.

How does God's directive to follow where He leads test the faith of His people?

THE TABERNACLE ERECTED (40:1–33)

Almost a year after the Passover, the Lord directs Moses to begin assembling the tabernacle from the various components the artisans have created. Each of the items for the tabernacle is put in place just as God has directed.

THE GLORY OF THE LORD (40:34–38)

The glory of the Lord in the cloud settles over the tabernacle. As long as the cloud remains on the tent, the Israelites remain in that location. When the cloud moves on, so do the people.

God's Glory Fills the Tabernacle

Every element of the tabernacle and its furnishings served to remind the people of God's presence with them. The golden lampstand gave light to the Holy Place, and the table for the bread of the Presence reminded the people of God's provision. At the altar of incense, the priests offered prayer for the people.

A finely woven curtain with images of cherubim (angels) separated the Holy Place from the Most Holy Place. The Most Holy Place contained the ark of the covenant with the mercy seat of God.

The extensive use of gold, as well as symbols like pomegranates and almond blossoms, served not only to remind the people of the glory of heaven but also to refer back to the Garden of Eden, which was lost to them but which God will restore to His people through Christ in the new creation.

LEVITICUS

Welcome to Leviticus

Leviticus, the third book of Moses, lays out the procedures for worship and living that God establishes for His people, Israel, after the tabernacle had been built and established. It is named for the tribe of Levi, from which Moses and his brother, Aaron, the first high priest of Israel, came.

Leviticus describes specific procedures for the sacrifices, anointing and installing the priesthood of Aaron and his sons, and the festivals God designed for His people. The sacrifices and festivals point squarely to the redeeming work that Jesus Christ, our great High Priest and the Lamb of God, would do roughly 1,500 years later for all humanity when He was sacrificed on the cross for the forgiveness of all our sins. As you read this book, think of the holy demands of God, which Jesus met perfectly, giving you access to God the Father through His suffering, death, and resurrection.

What are your first impressions of Leviticus? What comes to mind when you think of this book? What do you already know? What do you think you could learn more about?

Leviticus at a Glance

- **Start:** Leviticus begins with a manual to guide the priests for the various offerings God established for His people.

- **End:** Leviticus ends with various moral laws that will govern how the community of Israelites lives together.

- **Theme:** God cleanses, atones, and redeems His people so they may find rest and joy in His presence among them.

- **Author and Date:** The prophet Moses wrote Leviticus, likely while Israel camped at Mount Sinai around 1445 BC.

- **Places Visited:** Mount Sinai

- **Journey Time:** The twenty-seven books of Leviticus can be read in about two hours.

- **Outline:**
  - Manual of Offerings (1:1–7:38)
  - Ordination into the Priesthood (8:1–10:20)
  - Manual of Purity (11:1–15:33)

Five Top Sights and Spectacles of Leviticus

The Various Offerings (1:1–7:38) Watch as God reveals aspects of Jesus' future great sacrifice on the cross in the various offerings prescribed for Israel. Especially significant is the peace offering, because all Israelites eat the meat of the sacrifice in communion with God and the priests. Jesus gives us His own body and blood in Holy Communion to assure us our sins are forgiven and we are at peace with God.

The Consecration of Aaron and His Sons (8:1–9:24) Over seven days, God ordains Aaron and his sons, preparing them to serve as His priests on the eighth day. It reminds us of Jesus' last week on earth, when He died on the sixth day, rested on the seventh, and rose on the eighth to sit at God's right hand as our great eternal High Priest.

Laws concerning Leprosy and Cleansing Lepers (13:1–14:57) Later, when Jesus would heal lepers, He often directed them to go to the priests and fulfill these directives so the priests would see that Jesus was genuine.

The Day of Atonement (16:1–34) This is the high point of Leviticus. Every autumn, God provides a festival that prefigures what Jesus would one day accomplish on Good Friday. When coupled with the spring Passover, the Day of Atonement gives Israel glimpses into the type of sacrifice that Jesus would accomplish.

The Feasts of the Lord (23:1–44) God establishes Israel's worship calendar, every part of which reminds His people that He created the world, provides for their physical needs, and cleanses their sins through the promised Savior.

Seeing Jesus in Leviticus

Leviticus can be a difficult book to read because it seems like a manual of worship for the priests—which it is. But the worship God establishes for His people focuses squarely on looking forward to the promised

Savior and the sacrifice Jesus would make on the cross to purify us from our sins. Every sacrifice, every directive, every festival points to the work Jesus would accomplish during His life, death, and resurrection.

 **SET THE SCENE**

When and where did Moses receive the contents of Leviticus?

At the close of Exodus, Moses assembled the tent of meeting, and the glory of the Lord lifted from Mount Sinai and entered the tabernacle. Because of the glory of the Lord, Moses was unable to enter the tent of meeting. In the opening verse of Leviticus, God summoned Moses, permitting him to enter the tent of meeting, where God began instructing him on how Israel would be able to live in His presence.

No longer did Israel have to travel to Mount Sinai, the mountain of the Lord, to see the glory of the Lord. It was now dwelling with them in the tent of meeting. No longer would Moses have to climb Mount Sinai to speak with God; God spoke to him face to face in the tent of meeting.

God established the priesthood in Israel. He laid out the system of worship, sacrifices, and festivals by which the people of Israel were purified to approach Him. These appointed procedures, recorded in Leviticus, also pointed ahead to Jesus' sacrifice on the cross and the forgiveness, peace, and joy God gives us through His Word and Sacraments today.

Manual of Offerings (1:1–7:38)

The first seven chapters are instructions to the priests on how to offer the various offerings God commands. Each offering reveals different aspects of Jesus' great sacrifice on the cross to satisfy God's wrath and remove the sins of all people. Chapters 1–3 discuss voluntary offerings that pleased God. Chapters 4–5 detail offerings that were required to atone for sins. Chapters 6–7 describe offerings that were to be eaten by the priests and the Israelites.

LAWS FOR BURNT OFFERINGS (1:1–17)

In order for our holy God to accept sinners into His presence, a whole animal is sacrificed, producing an aroma that pleases God. It is necessary that the animal, which could have been a young male bull or bird, is clean and without blemish so that it stands in pure contrast to the family's uncleanness in sin. In the same way, Jesus, the Lamb of God, would one day be sacrificed on the cross so God the Father could accept us into His presence in heaven.

 LINK BETWEEN THE TESTAMENTS

Worship: A Gift for All God's People (Galatians 3:27–29)

Contrary to the practice of the false religions surrounding Israel, God ordained that all people would be able to worship Him in the ways that He set forth in Leviticus. Throughout the book, God referred these worship instructions not just to the priests (who in other religions at that time commonly hoarded such knowledge) but also to "the people of Israel," meaning all of God's people. God's common gift continues in the New Testament promise of Christ and expands further when Paul exhorts the Galatians, saying, "For as many of you as were baptized into Christ have put on Christ. There is neither Jew nor Greek, there is neither slave nor free, there is no male and female, for you are all one in Christ Jesus. And if you are Christ's, then you are Abraham's offspring, heirs according to promise" (Galatians 3:27–29). Jesus' grace was not the special inheritance of any one special group, nor was it the jealously guarded secret of a few. God came down to Mount Sinai to gather His people into a community centered around worship, and He continues to gather His people into a community of believers from every nation, people, and language.

Why do you think God was so specific about which parts of the offering could be eaten after it was made?

LAWS FOR GRAIN OFFERINGS (2:1–16)

The Israelites bring freshly gathered grain in various states, burning it for the pleasing aroma and acceptance it would confer. Laypeople are permitted to offer either fine flour, roasted fresh grain, or unleavened bread combined with olive oil and frankincense in different ways. The presiding priest burns a portion on the altar to God, while the remainder becomes most holy and is then eaten by the priests in God's presence. The various grain offerings foreshadow the Sacrament of Holy Communion, when we eat the very body of Christ, our Savior.

LAWS FOR PEACE OFFERINGS (3:1–17)

For a peace offering, which is made most often during high holy days and special occasions, an Israelite is to lay hands on the sacrifice's head and confess sins. The sacrifice is then killed in the sinner's place and eaten by the priests, their families, and the Israelite family in the Lord's presence. The Israelites are reassured they have peace with God as they eat the very body of the sacrifice that has died in their place for their sins. This makes the peace offerings the clearest foretaste of Holy Communion among Israel's sacrifices.

LAWS FOR SIN OFFERINGS (4:1–5:13)

When an Israelite commits an unintentional sin, that sin can be forgiven through a sin offering. Different animals and procedures are required depending on whether the sinner is a priest, the Israelite congregation as a whole, a leader, or an individual Israelite. But in each case, the blood of the sacrifice is sprinkled on the veil of the sanctuary or the bronze altar. Likewise, God would one day see Jesus' blood sprinkled on the cross and forgive and accept us sinners for Jesus' sake. Though not blood, the baptismal waters sprinkled on God's people today serve a similar role, cleansing and forgiving us sinners for Jesus' sake.

How might a sin offering lighten the heart of an Israelite weighed down by guilt? In what way is Confession and Absolution similar to a sin or guilt offering?

LAWS FOR GUILT OFFERINGS (5:14–6:7)

When a person commits a sin that breaks or damages his or her relationship with God or a neighbor, a guilt offering can be brought forward for reconciliation and forgiveness.

⊙ WAYPOINT

Israel's Offerings

What does this text show us?

In the opening chapters of Leviticus, we read about the kinds of offerings that God institutes for Israel to use as they worship Him. Each category of offering represents a different type of interaction with God, utilizes different elements and procedures, and results in certain, special outcomes for the worshipers involved. These offerings assure the Israelites that not a single one of their sins is beyond God's forgiveness and allow them to have communion with God through the atonement and blessing He offers in this key component of worship.

What similarities do you see between the types of offerings? How might this regularity be beneficial for God's people?

Where do you see examples of Christlike sacrifice in your daily life? How can you better emulate His sacrifice?

The apostle Paul describes our bodies as "temples," or houses for God (see 1 Corinthians 3:16–17). What ways can you keep your temple clean for Him?

What does this text reveal about God's plan of salvation?

God's rites of offering indicate the central feature of salvation: sacrifice. In order to rectify the punishment of death for the original sin of Adam and Eve, an innocent person has to die in the place of the sinner. God provides His people with a worship enacted through offering to give them access to this kind of substitution. Instead of dying themselves, they bring an unblemished animal to take their place upon the altar and be slaughtered so they can live by God's grace. Animal sacrifice, however, will not be enough; the effects do not last. In light of any new transgressions of the Law, the Israelites need to offer new sacrifices again and again thanks to humanity's fallen nature. Only God—who came down from heaven, became flesh, lived a perfect life, and died upon the altar of a cross to take upon Himself the sins of all mankind—could ever live up to the demands of the Law. And Jesus Christ did, offering Himself as the final unblemished sacrifice to break the power sin, death, and the devil held over us all.

What does this text uncover about our identity and calling as God's people today?

It might seem irrelevant for Christians who live in the eternal aftermath of Christ's death and resurrection to discuss the nuances of Israelite offering practices, but that view fails to recognize a critical element of our faith. The traditions and worship of Israel are just as much a part of our heritage and are what God used to prepare His people for the arrival and wonderful deeds of Jesus. The image of altar sacrifice is a helpful comparison to draw when discussing the crucifixion because it clearly conveys the gravity and necessity of what Jesus did. The wide variety of offerings God provided for His people reassures us that Jesus' suffering and death covers every one of our sins, no matter how unforgiveable they may seem in our eyes. We should honor all that God has done to achieve our salvation and give thanks for the immense grace we have received on account of God's even greater love for us.

THE PRIESTS AND THE OFFERINGS (6:8–7:38)

God describes the portions of animal sacrifice that the priests and their families are to eat and those that the Israelite people could eat. These offerings enable the priests and Levites to dedicate themselves to serving God's people full-time, just as our offerings enable our pastors and other church workers to minister to us full-time, as our gifts provide for their physical needs.

Ordination into the Priesthood (8:1–10:20)

God chooses Moses' brother, Aaron, to be Israel's first high priest. Aaron prefigures our great High Priest, Jesus Christ.

CONSECRATION OF AARON AND HIS SONS (8:1–36)

Mirroring Genesis 1, where God spends seven days creating the heavens and the earth, Moses spends seven days anointing Aaron as high priest and his sons as priests. Priests represent sinners before God. They offer the sacrifices that atone for the sins of the people. They represent God to the people by proclaiming God's acceptance of the sacrifice for the forgiveness of their sins. Jesus is our great High Priest, who sacrificed His own body and blood on the cross to atone for our sins and win our forgiveness.

 PICTURE OF THE SAVIOR

Jesus, Our High Priest

God meticulously designed the role of Israel's priesthood, and in its careful construction lies a gleaming reflection of the Savior for God's people. The priests' primary role was to represent the people to God by offering sacrifices to redeem sins. They also led festivals celebrating God's wonderful deeds on their behalf. When performing his various duties, the high priest wore a vest called an ephod, which was embedded with twelve gems—one for each of the twelve tribes of Israel. His ordination process was also quite stringent. Because Aaron and his sons were all sinners, Moses had to offer many sacrifices and cleansing procedures to make them acceptable to stand and serve before God. After those sacrifices and cleansing, Aaron was sent to the entrance of the tabernacle tent, where he remained for seven days until he could begin his new role on the eighth day. Jesus was our ultimate priest, offering Himself as the final and perfect sacrifice so that the sins of all who believe—represented by the twelve tribes of Israel, the totality of believers—would be cleansed. On the eighth day of His Holy Week, Jesus rose from the dead and sits as our High Priest at the right hand of God the Father.

Where have you seen evidence of God working through the monetary offerings His people give back to Him?

How would you feel if you were one of Aaron's sons and Nadab and Abihu were struck down before you?

The LORD Accepts Aaron's Offering (9:1–24)

After a week of being consecrated and set apart from the other Israelites, Aaron offers his sacrifice on the eighth day, and God accepts it. Much later, Jesus was set aside from the other Jews when He rode into Jerusalem for His last week. After His death, He rose to life on the eighth day (Sunday), showing that God the Father had accepted His sacrifice for our sins and the sins of the world.

The Death of Nadab and Abihu (10:1–20)

 WAYPOINT

What does this text show us?

Aaron's two oldest sons, Nadab and Abihu, are struck dead when they disobey God's rules, burning incense in a way God had not authorized for them. Nadab and Abihu remind us that we cannot approach God any way we choose. We must approach Him through faith in Jesus Christ alone. Their deaths illustrate the great danger of twisting God's Word for our own purposes, no matter how small the infraction may seem in our eyes.

What does this text reveal about God's plan of salvation?

In His Word, God determines what is acceptable for the worship life of His people and expects us to observe and honor His guidelines. As it often does with the Law, however, our sinful nature seeks to find its own way and turn from God's design for our lives. Nadab and Abihu disregard the precise procedure God has taught them for burning incense. Moses does not clearly record if they cut corners out of laziness or added something foreign to God's instructions out of pride. Jesus said, "No one comes to the Father except through Me" (John 14:6). In our worship, we must show reverence for God's presence among us in the things He has commanded us: His Word and Sacraments. Oftentimes, we, like Nadab and Abihu, fail to honor God this way and condemn ourselves by our sins. Yet in His great mercy, Jesus took all our sins upon Himself and suffered, died, and rose again that we might be forgiven, even for our irreverent moments.

What does this text uncover about our identity and calling as God's people today?

God kills Nadab and Abihu in such an extreme way because they have dishonored the worship practices He has given them in favor of their own modified ways. The brothers do not respect the gift of worship God has given them and, in failing to do so, place themselves above God. In other words, God punishes them on account of the highest pride, which follows Satan's pattern of sin. We are called to honor and cherish the blessings of worship God has given us today—most notably His Word and Sacraments—and we should take care to revere God as we glorify Him, lest we fall into the same trap of glorifying ourselves instead.

What are some aspects of your worship life (prayer, devotion, attitude in worship) that could use some refining so that you can focus more clearly on God and His Word in your daily life?

Manual of Purity (11:1–15:33)

The first main section of Leviticus closes with five chapters discussing purity among Israel's people. God grants His people a reference guide to proper conduct as they seek to humbly offer Him sacrifices, to worship Him, and to live in His presence. This manual applied only to the Israelite people and belongs to the ceremonial law. It is not binding on Christians today.

Clean and Unclean Animals (11:1–47)

In order that His people might rightfully honor Him and avoid the fate of Nadab and Abihu, God regulates their diet. If anyone would eat an unclean animal for sustenance, that person would become defiled and die in such impurity. Thus, God clearly outlines which kinds of animals were clean and good for the Israelites to eat. Through these provisions, it is clear that living within the bounds of God's Word bestows many blessings, while life apart from God's Word brings only suffering and destruction.

What parameters did God set for the Israelites' diet? How would these parameters influence how you would go about gathering and preparing food?

VISUALIZE

What's Good to Eat?

God's Word lays out very specific dietary laws for the children of Israel. Some more-traditional Jewish believers still observe these dietary laws today.

CLEAN

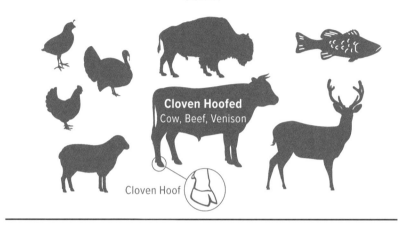

Cloven Hoofed
Cow, Beef, Venison

Cloven Hoof

UNCLEAN

Swine Flesh
Pig/Hog, Ham, Bacon, Pork

Is childbirth a neat and clean process? How does God provide for us in the midst of it?

PURIFICATION AFTER CHILDBIRTH (12:1–8)

God then describes how the process of childbirth makes a woman ceremonially unclean because of the flowing blood involved. God gives specific instructions for cleansing a mother who gave birth, including restrictions on where she may go and sacrifices she must offer to cleanse herself. The pains and troubles of childbirth are a consequence of sin (see Genesis 3:16), yet God shows His grace in offering His people restoration in these practices.

CLEAR THE CONFUSION

Does ceremonially unclean mean sinful?

Leviticus speaks about bodily discharges that made a person ceremonially unclean. These natural discharges were not sinful in and of themselves. But they provided a powerful object lesson to show the holiness God required for us to abide in His presence. Ceremonial uncleanness was a powerful reminder that none of us is holy, sinless, and pure. Since a single sin was enough to drive Adam and Eve from God's presence in the Garden of Eden, we have no hope to live in God's presence unless all our sins are cleansed in the blood of Jesus Christ, our Savior. The cleansing rituals God gave the priests offered worshipers the physical sensation of cleanness to remind them that God had forgiven their sins for the sake of the coming Savior.

What is God's tone in this section of the Scriptures? How does it compare with His dialogue in Genesis or Exodus? Why would it be helpful to understand this?

Laws About Leprosy (13:1–59)

At the time of Leviticus, leprosy is a very real danger to the physical well-being of God's people. It also provides an outward sign of the uncleanness that lurks in all hearts because of all people's sinful nature. The physical effects of leprosy remind Israelites of sin that continues to spread through their thoughts, words, and deeds. In Leviticus, God commands special procedures for identifying and handling the disease, even including temporary isolation for those who contract it, so that God could continue to dwell among His people.

Have you ever had to take care of someone so sick as to need to be isolated? Describe that experience.

 SET THE SCENE

What is leprosy?

Leprosy was a blanket term for several skin diseases. When the term is used in the Scriptures, however, it commonly refers to a specific skin disease. This disease made a person ceremonially unclean and inflicted chronic (long-lasting) infections that killed off the flesh and made it decay. It often broke through the skin and opened raw ulcers on the body. It also destroyed the hair follicles on infected parts of the body, causing the dark hair to become white or yellow and wispy.

Before a treatment was discovered in the 1940s, the only way to avoid contracting leprosy was to stay away from people who had the disease. As a result, many ancient societies banished those with leprosy from civilized life and left them to die and carry the sickness away with them. Interestingly, some cultures seemed not to banish lepers, as we see in the case of Naaman, the commander of the Syrian army who was cured by the prophet Elisha in 2 Kings 5.

Even today, many places around the world do not have access to proper treatment, and leprosy continues to afflict thousands of people in Africa and Southeast Asia. Despite all of the complicating factors, however, Jesus would go straight to many people suffering from leprosy and heal them, to the amazement of many, providing physical wellness that reflected their great faith in Him.

 VISUALIZE

Leprosy

LAWS FOR CLEANSING LEPERS (14:1–32)

Sometimes God intervenes directly and cures lepers of their leprosy. In those cases, God provides a means of purification by which lepers can be cleansed and restored to their place within Israelite society. These measures involve dutiful sacrifices, particular washing of the body, and dressing anew with holy oil, all done by the priest to ensure that the leper is clean before God after harboring the uncleanness of the skin disease. The duty of identifying leprosy, separating lepers from the community, and cleansing and restoring them is delegated to the priests by God. Later, when Jesus heals lepers in His public ministry, He often directs them to show themselves to the priests to authenticate the miracle.

CLEAR THE CONFUSION

Why did God place such severe restrictions around lepers?

God placed severe restrictions around lepers for both practical and theological reasons. Leprosy was a very communicable disease with no discernible cure at the time. To prevent the sickness from blazing through the entire population, God commanded that the lepers should be kept separate and away from those who were healthy. More importantly, though, leprosy was the most visible sign of sin's corruption. God sought to teach His people through the example of earthly sickness and, with smaller cleansing acts of the flesh, prepare them for the complete cleansing through Jesus Christ.

Laws for Cleansing Houses (14:33–57)

God commands that the houses that Israel would one day claim in conquest must be cleansed if found harboring leprosy. If the disease would persist beyond a very thorough cleansing and renewal process, the house would be deemed unclean and torn down, and its parts carried away to an unclean place.

LINK BETWEEN THE TESTAMENTS

Jesus Purifies Us in Baptism (Ephesians 4:22–24)

A major theme throughout the book of Leviticus is the uncleanness of God's people and the cleansing rites God provided for them. God specifically discusses lepers as the prominent outward sign of uncleanness, a visible reminder of sin's corruption. Sin makes us unclean and unable to be with God, since His complete purity and holiness abhor it. In order to rectify this in the short term, God made a way for people with leprosy to be cleansed and readmitted into life with Him among the Jews. This quick fix wouldn't solve the root issue of sin, however, so God sent His Son to address it once and for all. Paul helps us understand our new cleansing in his letter to the Ephesians: "You have heard about Him and were taught in Him . . . to put off your old self, which belongs to your former manner of life and is corrupt through deceitful desires, and to be renewed in the spirit of your minds, and to put on the new self, created after the likeness of God in true righteousness and holiness" (vv. 21–24). In Baptism, our sinful nature is drowned and replaced with one directed toward Christ and clothed in His righteousness. Christ has covered the uncleanness that once pervaded our lives so that, leprous or not, we are reconciled to God forever in faith.

Laws About Bodily Discharges (15:1–33)

God also gives cleanness laws beyond just foreign skin diseases, because the body itself could make an Israelite unclean before God. Under these laws, discharges from the body, both those that resulted from sickness and those naturally occurring through sexual intercourse and menstruation, make their source and everything they touch unclean for an entire day. Even in measures as stringent as these, God shows His love, for by these stipulations, His people could not engage in ritual prostitution on His behalf and were given mercy to love Him faithfully.

The Day of Atonement (16:1–34)

The Day of Atonement would take place in the fall of the year and foreshadow many features of Jesus' sacrifice on the cross, as we will see in the coming chapters. It would be the perfect counterpart to the spring festival of Passover, which also foreshadows Jesus' sacrifice as the Passover Lamb of God.

The Day of Atonement (16:1–34)

 WAYPOINT

How might the events listed in chapter 16 serve to bring Israel together under God's name each year?

How many connections can you find between the events of the Day of Atonement and what Jesus did on the cross for you?

What does this text show us?
This central chapter describes the high holy day of Israel's worship, noting the main features that must occur, step by step, in order for the congregation to be cleansed. First, the high priest enters the Most Holy Place and makes a sin offering for himself with a bull. Then he sacrifices the first of two goats as a guilt offering for the congregation, releasing the second goat into the wilderness after laying upon it the sins of Israel. For the rest of that day, no work should be done, providing a Sabbath of solemn rest.

What does this text reveal about God's plan of salvation?
Not only does the Day of Atonement emphasize the importance of sacrifice contained in all of the offerings, but it also highlights the centrality of God's love for humanity in His greater plan for salvation. God sets aside an entire day of the year purely for the purpose of cleansing His people. This cleansing isn't a neat or easy kind either. God took it upon Himself to enact the most effective measures for atonement so that He can dwell among His children. And this is only the beginning, for He has greater designs in mind. As Paul writes in his letter to the Romans, "For one will scarcely die for a righteous person—though perhaps for a good person one would dare even to die—but God shows His love for us in that while we were still sinners, Christ died for us" (Romans 5:7–8). God was willing to send His one and only Son to die on

our behalf. This is the ultimate sacrifice, the greatest love the world has ever known, which rests at the heart of our salvation.

What does this text uncover about our identity and calling as God's people today?

Just as the love of God is central to salvation, so, too, His love is at the center of our identity as Christians today. We live now and forevermore because of it, and, likewise, we are called to confess it by our words, actions, and relationships with the people God has placed in our lives. The Day of Atonement is a great snapshot of such love for us and points our hearts to the unfathomable grace we have been given in freedom from sin and new life in Christ. By this, we are reminded of the joy that we have in our salvation and are inspired to share it gladly with the world.

How are our lives as Christians both grounded and sustained by the atoning sacrifice of Christ? How can we continue to keep that act front and center in our identity as God's people?

 PICTURE OF THE SAVIOR

The Scapegoat

As the central part of the religious rites on the Day of Atonement, the scapegoat is one of the clearest images of Jesus found in the book of Leviticus. After sacrificing a bull for himself and a goat for the people, and consecrating the ark of the covenant with the blood of the sacrifices, the high priest would then lay his hands on a live goat and lay the sins of Israel upon it. Once he had pronounced all the sins onto the goat's head, he sent it away into the wilderness, where it was left to die. After Jesus' Baptism, John the Baptist referenced this scapegoat as he pointed to Jesus and said, "Behold, the Lamb of God, who takes away the sin of the world!" (John 1:29). At that time, Jesus was led into the wilderness by the Holy Spirit to be tempted by the devil. Christ carried those sins on Good Friday as He was our scapegoat, abandoned to die on the cross in order that we might be pure and innocent before God in eternity.

Place yourself in the shoes of an Israelite who was watching the events of the Day of Atonement unfold. What would you have seen, felt, and experienced?

Showing Reverence for the Sanctuary (17:1–22:33)

To open the second major section of Leviticus, God gives special instructions on how His people should conduct themselves in and around the sanctuary, the place where He dwells among them. Once again, there is a clear emphasis on remaining clean and pure with additional exhortations to hold fast to the Ten Commandments throughout daily life.

THE PLACE OF SACRIFICE (17:1–9)

In no uncertain terms, God commands that sacrifices must be brought before the tabernacle and offered at the entrance to the tent of meeting. If anyone sacrifices to God anywhere else and brings it to the tent only after, that person will be charged with bloodguilt and cut off from his people.

LAWS AGAINST EATING BLOOD (17:10–16)

Similarly, God abhors the consumption of blood and reckless slaughter of animals, instituting the same punishment of banishment for these crimes. Additionally, an animal already killed by other animals is deemed ceremonially unclean, and eating its meat conferred its uncleanness in the same manner as bodily discharges.

Why is the location of sacrifice and worship so important to God?

👑 PICTURE OF THE SAVIOR

The Power of Blood

While God's discourse on the treatment of blood in this chapter may seem quite crude to our modern sensibilities, it is important to recognize the enduring significance for our faith. Jesus shed His lifeblood on the cross so that our sinful, unclean hearts could be made as white as snow before God. His own blood is what Jesus has given to us for our continuous spiritual nourishment in the Lord's Supper, graciously given to the first disciples to seal the new covenant and to us under that same promise today. Only through Jesus' holy and precious blood have we been granted new life and freedom from the bondage of sin in this fallen world: "You were ransomed from the futile ways inherited from your forefathers, not with perishable things such as silver or gold, but with the precious blood of Christ, like that of a lamb without blemish or spot" (1 Peter 1:18–19).

Unlawful Sexual Relations (18:1–30)

God calls His people to a high standard of sexual purity in contrast to the hedonistic practices of the nations surrounding them and in order to preserve Israel's cleanness. Incestuous and homosexual relationships were and are strictly forbidden by God's Law. The intercourse preserved within the confines of God-ordained marriage is a gift to protect us from breaking the Sixth Commandment: "You shall not commit adultery" (Exodus 20:14).

 CLEAR THE CONFUSION

Is God still against homosexuality?

God created humans to be spiritual and physical creatures. He established His Commandments to safeguard both our spiritual and physical lives. Homosexuality violates the order God created and harms people physically, emotionally, and spiritually, just like every other sin. Acting upon sinful lusts of any kind outside of God's prescribed boundaries for sexuality (namely men and women in marriage) is unacceptable to God and a violation of the order He created.

By dismissing God's created order for human love and procreation to pursue carnal pleasure, homosexual relations sharply divide us from God. When we turn away from God in any way, we condemn ourselves to the punishment of sin—death and, in death, eternal separation from God. People may experience homosexual desires as a result of living in a broken world, but it is acting upon those desires, as if God's will does not matter, that is sin. The experience of homosexual desires is a powerful example of our corruption as fallen creatures, but so are gossip, lies, and slander. At the end of the day, we have all sinned and fallen short of God's glory (Romans 3:23). God calls us to see all people as those in need of His grace and redemption through Jesus. It should be our goal to share both the Law and Gospel with those around us, whether serial gossipers or those who act upon homosexual desires, so that God can work repentance and faith in their lives.

The LORD Is Holy (19:1–8)

God decrees that His people shall be a reflection of His holiness and reaffirms the covenant promise made atop Mount Sinai when Moses received the Commandments. Sacrifices are to be taken seriously and handled properly when they are offered.

What would happen to God's people in this time if they began to deviate from His boundaries for marriage and sexual relations? What happens to God's people today when we begin to deviate from what God designed for us in marriage and sexuality?

How is God's uncompromising language throughout Leviticus a comfort to the modern Christian?

What about Israelite society is different from our own? How might these rules help someone better love his or her neighbor?

LOVE YOUR NEIGHBOR AS YOURSELF (19:9–18)

God exhorts Israel to keep the second table of the Law in particular ways. Provisions for aiding the poor, matters of justice, and familial relations are all addressed.

YOU SHALL KEEP MY STATUTES (19:19–37)

Continuing the pattern set in the previous chapters, God establishes more statutes to set Israel apart from the surrounding idolatrous nations. By these commands, God's people are guarded from falling into many of the pitfalls of their neighbors: spiritual ambiguity, licentiousness, and malcontent toward outsiders.

 SET THE SCENE

What were the false gods of the other nations in Canaan like?

Canaan's false gods were many in number and quite different from the true God we know and love. They were often considered territorial—having dominion over a mountain, river, or other geographical area—in stark contrast to our God, who created the whole earth and rules over it (see Psalm 148). Additionally, each one typically had a single defining feature that shaped how followers would worship. These were some of the most commonly worshiped gods in the ancient Near East:

Baal, the chief deity in Canaanite culture, was thought to be the god of storms and fertility and had a female consort called **Ashtoreth**. These two, in particular, were a nasty blight on Israel in the time of the judges and all throughout the period of the divided kingdom.

Chemosh, a deity worshiped primarily by the Moabites, was likely a god of war and made several appearances in the lives of God's people, as recorded in 1 and 2 Kings.

Dagon, a deity favored by the Philistines, was often considered Baal's father, and he featured in the narrative of the judge Samson (Judges 16). He was shown to be powerless when the ark of the covenant was brought into his temple (1 Samuel 5).

Molech, a Canaanite god whose sacrificial worship was especially cruel, required the "offering" of young children and infants for his satisfaction. God found worship of Molech highly detestable and instituted the harshest punishments for those who dared blaspheme Him in this way.

These false gods might seem outrageous to us, yet in some ways, they are quite similar to many of our modern idols. We continue to wander astray with popular false gods such as money, power, fame, and sexual immorality.

Canaanite Idol

What are some other idols that our society exalts? How can you best defend yourself against their influence?

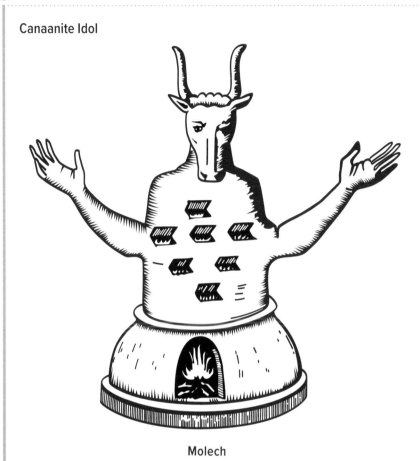

Molech

Punishment for Child Sacrifice (20:1–9)

God condemns to death all who practice child sacrifice in Israel, whether kin or strangers. He sets firm boundaries so that His people are faithful to Him alone and do not wander astray with false gods and enticing deceptions of the world.

Punishments for Sexual Immorality (20:10–21)

Having instituted His strict commands for sexual purity in chapter 18, God orders the harshest punishments for those who practice immoral sexual relations. In the eyes of the world, these consequences would preserve the holiness of God's name as it was borne by His people.

From this text, and from elsewhere in the Bible, why do you suppose that God treated child sacrifice as the most detestable of sins? What does this show us about who God is and what He thinks of His human creatures?

VISUALIZE

Punishment by Stone or Banishment: A Grisly Sight

Stoning as a form of the death penalty is first recorded in the Books of Moses. Acts 7:54–60 reports the stoning of the first Christian martyr, Stephen. This fresco from a church in Prague depicts this event.

Stoning as a form of capital punishment is still practiced in some Islamic states in the Middle East. This punishment is most frequently assigned for those who have committed adultery.

The size of stones used are selected so as to cause injury but not bring about death too quickly. The condemned may be placed into a hole and partially buried, making it difficult, if not impossible, to escape from the punishment. In this case, if the person somehow escapes the hole, the stoning stops and the person is released. Human rights groups are working with government leaders around the world to abolish this brutal form of punishment.

What details stand out to you in this section? How has your mental image of holiness changed after reading this part of Leviticus?

How does the contrast between God's promises of blessing and of judgment reveal who He is?

YOU SHALL BE HOLY (20:22–27)

God carefully reminds His people that they are made holy not by their perfect adherence to His commands but only by grace alone. It is out of love that God directs Israel away from the self-destructive practices of the idolaters around them, and so, too, does God call us through the Gospel of Jesus Christ into the freedom from sin to honor Him.

HOLINESS AND THE PRIESTS (21:1–22:16)

Moving His attention from the congregation at large to the clergy in particular, God distinguishes His priests as God's representatives among His people. Thus, it is necessary for their cleanness and purity to be safeguarded very carefully so that the tragedy of Nadab and Abihu will not repeat itself.

CLEAR THE CONFUSION

What does it mean to be holy?

We have seen God use the word *holy* numerous times in Leviticus, so while the context can provide some clarity to its meaning, it would be wise to zoom in further to investigate this word closely. At its root, *holy* is about separation of what is common (only connected to earthly things) from what is sacred (specially connected to the divine). When applied to God, holiness exists in its highest sense; God is holy and thus transcendent to everything else, morally excellent and pure in His entirety, and intimately tied to all that He has created, especially the human creatures He made in His own image. In other words, being holy is the essence of God's character. Therefore, when God speaks of applying holiness to humanity, a good way to understand this is twofold: our redemption, cleansing, and return to His "above-ness" by grace and our call to higher living among a common world as His goodness works a lifetime of turning back to Him in our hearts.

In what are other times and places in the Bible is God's holiness emphasized? How do these relate to how God talks about holiness in this section?

ACCEPTABLE OFFERINGS (22:17–33)

As with the priests themselves, the offerings they bring must have shared in purity. Disfigurement or other deformities disqualify sacrificial livestock. Appropriately, the animal for sacrifice must meet all of God's requirements or else whoever offers it will have failed to keep God's command. This also points ahead to Jesus' complete holiness and purity, making Him a perfect, spotless sacrifice who, since He had no sins of His own to pay for, could fully pay for all of our sins by His suffering and death.

Observing the Sabbath (23:1–27:34)

After structuring life around the appointed place of worship, God broadens His scope, and He details faithful life throughout one's days. The Third Commandment, "Remember the Sabbath day, to keep it holy" (Exodus 20:8), is a special concern, and God provides guidelines to help His people honor the command with full understanding.

FEASTS OF THE LORD (23:1–2)

God prescribes various festivals for special times of worship in all of Israel, each with its own remembrances and practices. All celebrations are given the highest priority and contain the command to rest, not work, during a special time of worship.

What is your most memorable holiday? What makes it so special for you?

How are each of the feasts the same? Which looks the most interesting to you? Why?

What do the insights of the festivals show us about God's character? What do they say about His relationship with mankind?

 VISUALIZE

Israel's Celebrations

In Genesis 2 and Exodus 20, the Lord hallowed the seventh day as a day of rest so that God's people could learn of and celebrate God's blessings and be strengthened for further service. During the exodus, the Lord added other feasts (Exodus 12; 23:10–19; 34:18–26) and required the men of Israel to gather annually for special celebrations. In this way, the Lord hallowed time so the people could share in His holiness. This chart gives an overview of the feasts as listed in Leviticus 23 and how the people observed them at the tabernacle.

REFERENCE	DATE	OCCASION	LAY OBSERVANCE	WORK PROHIBITION	OFFERING/ GIFTS TO THE LORD
23:3	Sabbath			Total	
23:5	14th day of first month	Passover			
23:6, 8	15th–21st days of first month	Feast of Unleavened Bread	Eating of unleavened bread		Yes
23:6–8	15th day of first month	First day of Feast of Unleavened Bread, a holy day	Eating of unleavened bread	Partial	Yes
23:8	21st day of first month	Last day of Feast of Unleavened Bread, a holy day	Eating of unleavened bread	Partial	Yes
23:9–14	16th day of first month	Feast of Firstfruits	Presenting the first sheaf of barley harvest		Yes
23:15–21	50th day after elevation of first sheaf	Feast of Weeks, a holy day (Day of Pentecost)		Partial	Yes
23:24–25	First day of seventh month	Feast of Trumpets, a holy day		Partial	Yes
23:27–32	10th day of seventh month	Day of Atonement, a holy day	Fasting	Total	Yes
23:34–43	15th–21st days of seventh month	Feast of Booths, Feast of the Lord, holy days	Going on pilgrimage, residing in booths, rejoicing		Yes
23:35	15th day of seventh month	First day of Feast of Booths, a holy day	Going on pilgrimage, residing in booths, rejoicing	Partial	Yes
23:36	22nd day of seventh month	Closing ceremony of Feast of Booths, a holy day		Partial	Yes

Start of Israelite year

As Jews, the earliest Christians followed the Israelite calendar and its feasts as observed by first-century Judaism. However, as more and more Gentiles came to faith in Jesus as their Savior, a new yearly pattern of worship emerged: the Church Year, which most Christians continue to observe today. The Israelite year was organized around the rhythm of the agricultural seasons in Israel and national events. By contrast, the Church Year was organized around the life and teachings of Jesus.

Two church festivals descend directly from Israelite feast days: Easter and Pentecost. For centuries, the early Christians referred to Easter as Pasch, from the Hebrew word for Passover. The name Pentecost comes from the Greek word for fifty, since Israelites and Christians celebrated this feast fifty days after Passover. These annual celebrations remind us of the Old Testament roots of the church as well as the transformation of worship in view of the life, death, and resurrection of Jesus. Study the chart below to grow in your understanding of the Jewish and Christian calendars.

With whom do you celebrate your most memorable holiday? How do those people change the meaning of the day?

OT AND JEWISH FEASTS	CELEBRATION	SEASON	CHURCH YEAR	CELEBRATION
Start of Israelite year/Rosh Hashanah Lv 23:23–25; Nu 29:1–6	Completion of agricultural year and beginning of new year	September/ October	Sundays after Pentecost	During the "Half-Year of the Church" (*Semester Ecclesiae*), worship focuses on the teaching of Jesus for the church.
Day of Atonement/ Yom Kippur Lv 16; 23:26–32; Nu 29:7–11	A day of national fasting and sacrifice during which the high priest entered the Most Holy Place in the tabernacle	September/ October		
Booths/Tabernacles/ Ingathering Ex 23:16; Lv 23:33–43; Nu 29:12–39; Dt 16:13–17	Harvest and commemoration of Israelite wanderings	September/ October		
Hanukkah Mentioned in Jn 10:22 as the Feast of Dedication	Purification of the temple from Seleucid rulers (165–164 BC)	December	Start of the Church Year Advent/ Christmas	The "Half-Year of the Lord" (*Semester Domini*) focuses on the life of Jesus.
Purim Est 9:18–32	National deliverance through Queen Esther at time of Babylonian exile	February/ March	Epiphany	
Passover/ Unleavened Bread Ex 12; 23:15; Nu 9; Dt 16:1–8	National redemption from Egypt	March/April	Lent/Easter	
Weeks/Pentecost/ Harvest Lv 23:15–22; Nu 28:26–31; Dt 16:9–12	Firstfruits of the wheat harvest	May/June	Ascension/ Pentecost	

🔗 LINK BETWEEN THE TESTAMENTS

A Reminder of the Greatest Promise (Colossians 2:16–17)

The heritage created in the ardent practice of these festivals became a connection point for Jews when they suffered greatly under future occupations and even exile. In this, the festivals served as wonderful forms of worship for those living in the promise of a Messiah yet to come. Nevertheless, the celebrations were never meant to last but were designed to prepare God's people for that very Messiah they awaited: Jesus Christ. Paul crystallized as much in his letter to the Colossians, writing, "Therefore let no one pass judgment on you in questions of food and drink, or with regard to a festival or a new moon or a Sabbath. These are a shadow of the things to come, but the substance belongs to Christ." Jesus' death and resurrection were the unspoken conclusion to hundreds of years of Jewish custom that brought about a new hope for God's people. No longer would they wait eagerly for a Savior and remember God's promise by feasts and rites, for His coming and sacrifice fulfilled God's great promise of salvation.

THE SABBATH (23:3)

God begins with the weekly celebration of the Sabbath. This falls on Saturday, the seventh day in which God rested from His labors of creating the heavens and the earth. His people are to rest from their labors each week to gather before Him and let Him serve them.

THE PASSOVER (23:4–8)

Each year, Israel will remember the tenth plague by eating the Passover lamb and recalling how God delivered Israel from Egypt on the night He killed the firstborn of Egypt and passed over the houses marked with blood of the lamb. This festival points ahead to Jesus, the Lamb of God, who marks us with His blood in Baptism.

THE FEAST OF FIRSTFRUITS (23:9–14)

The Israelites are to bring the firstfruits of their harvest to wave before God as a reminder that He provides all their food. This feast points ahead to the day of our Lord Jesus' resurrection, the firstfruits of those who have fallen asleep (1 Corinthians 15:20).

THE FEAST OF WEEKS (23:15–22)

Fifty days after the Feast of Firstfruits, Israel is to gather to celebrate the wheat harvest God has provided them. This feast is also known as Pentecost, named after the fifty days. It points ahead to the first harvest of souls, when Christ poured out the Spirit upon His disciples.

THE FEAST OF TRUMPETS (23:23–25)

This feast marks the beginning of the seventh month in Israel's calendar. The blast of trumpets celebrates the reign of God as Israel's King. A close New Testament parallel is the Sunday on which Christ enters Jerusalem in triumph, riding on a donkey, and the people proclaim Him David's Son, the King of Israel.

THE DAY OF ATONEMENT (23:26–32)

God set aside this day each year for the high priest to enter the Most Holy Place and sprinkle blood on the ark of the covenant to atone for the sinfulness of Israel. It points ahead to Good Friday, when Jesus came before His heavenly Father with the blood He shed on the cross to atone for our sins and the sins of all people.

THE FEAST OF BOOTHS (23:33–44)

This feast recalls Israel's travels through the wilderness from Egypt to the Promised Land. The people would recall how God provided all their needs until He brought them faithfully to the Promised Land.

THE LAMPS (24:1–4)

The Lord commands Israel to provide pure olive oil for the seven lamps in the lampstand or menorah. These lamps light up the interior of the Holy Place in the Tabernacle and reflect God's holiness.

BREAD FOR THE TABERNACLE (24:5–9)

God commands twelve loaves of bread to be baked each Sabbath Day and placed on the table of pure gold in the Holy Place in the Tabernacle. These represented each of the tribes of Israel. The priests were to eat the bread when it was removed at the end of the week. (David would eat of this bread when he first fled from King Saul in 1 Samuel 21, an action Jesus commended in Matthew 12:1–8.)

Based on the description in the text, what do you think the lamps and the bread would have looked like? What would the interior of the tabernacle have looked like from the perspective of a priest standing in its midst?

👑 PICTURE OF THE SAVIOR

The Light of the World and the Bread of Life

Jesus supplants both of these necessary parts of worship for the priests who commune with the Father in the tent of meeting. He illuminates the darkness of the world for mankind, bringing clarity and understanding to their deeds and inviting them into the brightness of a new life, just as the lamps helped the priests to see what they were doing as they served God. John writes in his Gospel, "To all who did receive Him, who believed in His name, He gave the right to become children of God, who were born, not of blood nor of the will of the flesh nor of the will of man, but of God" (John 1:12–13).

Jesus also gives life through the eternal sustenance of His body offered in the Lord's Supper: "Whoever feeds on My flesh and drinks My blood has eternal life, and I will raise him up on the last day. For My flesh is true food, and My blood is true drink. Whoever feeds on My flesh and drinks My blood abides in Me, and I in him" (John 6:54–56). The bread of the Presence, having once been a gift for the consecration of priests, is now gladly given for the forgiveness of sins to all who abide by Jesus' marvelous light.

When has God's name been an important anchor for you? Why should we do our best not to dishonor it?

PUNISHMENT FOR BLASPHEMY (24:10–16)

In a brief digression from Moses' account of God's instruction, the book of Leviticus describes an episode when an Israelite born to an Egyptian father blasphemes God's name before Israel. God will not stand mockery of His name, and because the man does so, he condemns himself to a curse from God and death by the hands of the Israelites.

 CLEAR THE CONFUSION

Isn't stoning the blasphemer too severe?

With freedom of speech the norm in many countries of the world today, God's sentence of stoning for this blasphemer can be shocking. But his sin was actually as severe as that of Nadab and Abihu, who desecrated the tabernacle by offering unauthorized incense. The priests could approach God's presence in the tabernacle by burning incense. When Nadab and Abihu broke God's rule, they desecrated the tabernacle and jeopardized the approach by all the other priests.

The Israelites had access to God through His personal name, Yahweh ("I AM"). But if that name was cursed and denigrated by being blasphemed, there was danger that God's name would no longer be holy to the Israelites and they would lose that special access to their God. And if they refused to put away the one who had blasphemed God's name, then God would have withdrawn access to His name and punished the entire nation.

This underscores the importance of the Second Commandment, "You shall not take the name of the LORD your God in vain, for the LORD will not hold him guiltless who takes His name in vain" (Exodus 20:7). Jesus has this same thinking in mind when He teaches us to pray "hallowed be Your name" (Matthew 6:9). For if God's name loses its holiness, who will call upon Him to be saved? That should make every Christian careful not to speak God's name mindlessly or as a curse, which teaches nonbelievers around us that Jesus Christ and God our Father are not really that important to us.

An Eye for an Eye (24:17–23)

Immediately following God's sentence of stoning, God establishes a principle of justice for Israel, summed up by the phrase "an eye for an eye." Less severe offenses will be punished more mildly than more severe offenses. In order to stave off vengeance in His people, God creates a system in which offenses are punished in the proper degree, and the lives of all people are to be held in the highest regard, just as the personal name of God is to be held in highest regard.

 VISUALIZE

Israel's Justice System

The Israelite system of justice was based on the principle of "an eye for an eye." Essentially, the guilty party made restitution equal to the loss suffered by the victim of the crime. For example, if a person caused another person to lose a goat, then the first person needed to provide another goat for the victim. Moses, or another designated leader, served as judge between the two.

The Sabbath Year (25:1–7)

Returning to God's decrees for Israel, Moses records God's concern for the vitality of the land and its bounty as Israel will settle upon it from place to place. God institutes a Sabbath year to allow the land rest after six years of hard work from Israel's farming and herding. This seventh year of rest will allow the Israelites to focus on God—trusting Him to provide their physical needs as they take a year off from farming—and be reminded that "man does not live by bread alone, but man lives by every word that comes from the mouth of the LORD" (Deuteronomy 8:3).

The Year of Jubilee (25:8–22)

Not only is there to be a Sabbath year for every six that passes but also there is to be a year of jubilee after the end of the seventh Sabbath year (the fiftieth year). The year of jubilee, held one year after the seventh Sabbath year, is to be a time of celebrating, freedom, and redemption for the Israelites, who receive all the blessings of the Sabbath year and even more through the return of land and freedoms gained from servanthood. This year of jubilee prefigures the entire New Testament era, after Jesus won freedom and forgiveness for all people, and points ahead to His return, when we will live with Him in freedom and celebration forever.

What does God tell us about our relationship with the world He created in the first part of chapter 25?

In what ways is the Christian Church Year calendar similar to and different from Israel's worship calendar?

How did Israel's worship calendar help focus Israel on God's plan of salvation? How does the Christian worship calendar accomplish the same thing?

How can you honor the holy days of the Christian calendar in a way that helps to share the Good News with the people in your life? Brainstorm some ideas.

WAYPOINT

Israel's Worship Calendar

What does this text show us?
God describes the liturgical calendar for Israel's special times of worship in great detail. God paints a clear picture of every festival He saw fit for Israel to celebrate by including the times of the year when each should be observed, what special worship practice should occur, whether God's people should work, and which offerings should be given.

What does this text reveal about God's plan of salvation?
God attaches a great deal of significance to tradition and the memory of His great works in Israel's history. On these days of feasting and rest from work, God calls His people to recall all that He has done for them through specific times in their past, and ultimately, that He keeps His promises. Inasmuch as these festivals point back in time to God's goodness, they also peer into the future to the anticipation of the fulfillment of God's greatest promise of salvation. Remembering God's nature necessitates remembering His grace for mankind immediately after the fall in the Garden of Eden, when He promised, "I will put enmity between you and the woman, and between your offspring and her offspring; He shall bruise your head, and you shall bruise His heel" (Genesis 3:15). The reminders of the individual festivals themselves are lovely and necessary on their own, but when taken as a whole, the summary of God's grace appears in the shining image of Jesus Christ.

What does this text uncover about our identity and calling as God's people today?
We recognize many seasons of celebration and holidays alike in the Christian calendar—Advent, Epiphany, Holy Week, Easter, Pentecost, and many more. As we honor these important times with special worship services, food, and commemorations of our own, let us not forget that it is Jesus Christ to whom they point. Though the world may try to adopt watered-down versions for its own use, we can remember and share the true, deeper meaning found in Jesus Christ as we celebrate Him in all kinds of ways across time and cultural boundaries.

REDEMPTION OF PROPERTY (25:23–34)

God clarifies the property-redeeming practice of which He spoke when establishing the year of jubilee, and He sets rules for how Israelites can buy back land they sold in difficult times. In this way, God preserves the valuable gift of land ownership in the individual families of Israel.

KINDNESS FOR POOR BROTHERS (25:35–46)

Returning to His discussion of the poor in Israelite society, God sets guidelines for how His people are to treat the less fortunate Israelites among them. God commands the Israelites to lend freely to their neighbors without charging interest or gaining a profit. They can employ them as hired hands but not as slaves.

REDEEMING A POOR MAN (25:47–55)

God sets guidelines for how a poor Israelite who has sold himself to a stranger or sojourner can be redeemed or bought back by a close relative or with his own money if he grows rich. God emphasizes the fraternal bond among Israel and the importance of honoring it in all circumstances of material wealth, for all good things come only through Him by grace.

 **SET THE SCENE**

How well did poor and rich people get along in ancient societies?

As many societies experience today, economic differences among people created a wide rift between members of a society. In ancient Near East societies like those found in Canaan, urban revolutions had resulted in a political shift toward kinship as opposed to territory alone. Additionally, a social shift had taken place that emphasized a sharp class division between the ruling elite—made up of military, religious, and political leaders who imposed tributes and taxes—and the largely agrarian lower class. These factors led to a natural animosity between the wealthy and poor in most societies. God's command for not only tolerance but also fraternity among His people regardless of their material wealth was yet another distinguishing sign that set Israel apart from the sinful nations surrounding them in the Promised Land.

BLESSINGS FOR OBEDIENCE (26:1–13)

On the one hand, God reminds Israel of His covenant promise—that by walking in His presence in faith in Him alone, they will receive many great blessings from Him. Only by His provision and steadfast care had they escaped Egypt and come thus far, and so it would be for the rest of their days.

Where do you see the continued promises of salvation in Leviticus?

PUNISHMENT FOR DISOBEDIENCE (26:14–46)

On the other hand, God also warns Israel of His equally wrathful punishment for them if they spurn Him and break His covenant. Pulling no punches, God describes the brutality and utter desolation He would bring to Israel in such a case, which would unfortunately come to pass soon after God brought them to the Promised Land.

How did God use the monetary gifts of His people in the Old Testament to sustain proper worship? How does God bless you today through tithes and offerings to the church?

LAWS ABOUT VOWS (27:1–34)

The closing chapter in Leviticus concludes the book with God's statutes for vows and offerings of the Israelites. Criteria for valuation included one's ability to work or produce, the specifics for a type of offering, and rules regarding their collection and safe care. These vows sustain the fund for maintenance of the tent of meeting and tabernacle and illustrate Israel's response to God's grace shown throughout the entire book of Leviticus.

 VISUALIZE

Laws About Vows

The book of Leviticus closes with this summary of the "vows," or voluntary offerings, the Israelites made for the care and maintenance of the tabernacle. The chart below outlines the vow amounts assigned to individuals. Animals brought for offerings were also assigned values depending on the condition and class of the animal. Animals given for sacrifice helped to support the priests. Some animals, given as a vow, could be redeemed or bought back. The redemption price helped support the tabernacle.

Male, age 20–60 years	50 shekels
Female, age 20–60 years	30 shekels
Male, age 5–20 years	20 shekels
Female, age 5–20 years	10 shekels
Male, age 1 month–5 years	5 shekels
Female, age 1 month–5 years	3 shekels
Male, age 60+ years	15 shekels
Female, age 60+ years	10 shekels
Poor male or female	Amount assigned by priests
Animals for sacrifice	May not be redeemed
Unclean animal	Amount assigned by priest +20%
Home*	Amount assigned +20%
Fields*	Amount based on yield
Firstborn clean animal	Dedicated to the Lord
Firstborn unclean animal	Amount assigned +20%
Tithe of the land (seed/fruit)	Value +20%

*Homes and fields reverted back to the original owner during the Year of Jubilee.

NUMBERS

Welcome to Numbers

The book of Numbers picks up the action after God's people have been camped at the mountain for about a year. Now a mighty nation, with a divinely organized army ready to conquer, the people journey toward Canaan. On the border, they lose confidence in God and plan a mutiny against God and Moses. Their punishment is another forty years of wandering in the Sinai wilderness until that generation of fighting men dies off. In those long years, God refines them for their task ahead, and the new generation born and raised in the wilderness learns to trust the Lord better than did their parents. The book ends on the border of the Promised Land, with God's people poised for conquest. The book of Numbers is a book of journeys, both geographically and spiritually, as God provides for His people despite the obstacles they encounter and their repeated lack of trust in Him. Join God's people in their sojourning and learn how God involves you in the journey of faith.

What do you know about the book of Numbers? What are some questions you have about this book and where it fits in God's plan of salvation?

Numbers at a Glance

- **Start:** Numbers begins around the year 1445 BC with God's people getting ready to leave Mount Sinai.

- **End:** Numbers ends with God's people getting ready to enter the Promised Land, around 1406 BC.

- **Theme:** Numbers describes how the Lord preserved His people despite the various obstacles they encountered and sins they committed on their way from Mount Sinai to the Promised Land.

- **Author and Date:** The prophet Moses wrote Numbers, likely during Israel's wilderness wanderings, between 1446 BC and 1406 BC.

- **Places Visited:** Mount Sinai, the Sinai Wilderness, Canaan

- **Journey Time:** The thirty-six chapters of Numbers can be read in about three hours.

- **Outline:**
  - From Mount Sinai to the Promised Land (1:1–6:27)
  - Consecrating the Tabernacle (7:1–12:16)
  - From the Promised Land to the Wilderness (13:1–14:45)
  - Religious Questions (15:1–19:22)
  - Journey Back toward the Promised Land (20:1–21:35)
  - Preparing to Enter the Promised Land (22:1–25:18)
  - The Second Census and New Laws (26:1–27:23)
  - God Confirms Offering Practices (28:1–30:16)
  - The Defeat of Midian (31:1–32:42)
  - The Final Preparations (33:1–36:13)

Five Top Sights and Spectacles of Numbers

The Encampment of God's People (2:1–34) Observe God's people as He organizes their camp and leads them out from Mount Sinai, and imagine what the mighty traveling city might have looked like with God's presence in the center and the mighty pillar leading them.

The People Refuse (13:1–14:45) Experience the fear and distrust of God's people as they see the might of Canaan and turn against Moses. As Moses intercedes before God, rejoice at God's mercy and grace to preserve His promises.

Korah's Rebellion (16:1–50) With Moses, endure the ongoing rebellion of the Levite Korah and his family as they attempt to assume control. Gaze in awe as God judges Korah and the other rebels for their sin by opening the ground, which then swallows them up.

The Bronze Serpent (21:4–9) Consider God's judgment against sin and mercy on sinners through this powerful episode, which Jesus Himself later pointed to as a picture of what He would do on the cross.

Balaam's Talking Donkey! (22:1–41) Marvel as God uses a pagan soothsayer, and his donkey, to show His unrelenting faithfulness to keep His promises to His people as they prepare to enter the Promised Land.

Seeing Jesus in Numbers

The book of Numbers chronicles the journey of God's people throughout the bulk of their wilderness wanderings. When we read these accounts, it's easy for us to see just how dependent the Israelites were on God's provision in everything. Food, water, preservation, and protection were all provided by God's direct hand over those forty years. Throughout it all, God was present in their midst—guiding and directing them through a pillar of cloud and fire, displaying His presence on the rock that provided water, and standing in the way of Balaam's donkey, among other things. Each of these physical appearances of God in the midst of the people, known as theophanies, points us to Jesus. Throughout the history of the church, biblical scholars have usually interpreted these direct appearances as the actual appearance of the Second Person of the Trinity, the Son of God, before He was born on earth. Not only that but these appearances also show us God's judgment against sin and His mercy to forgive and restore sinners. This is nowhere more evident than in the account of the bronze serpent, which Jesus Himself said pointed to Him and what He would do for the salvation of the world. This same Jesus who ascended into heaven is with His people always, to the end of the age, through the presence of the Spirit. Just as the Son of God was present with His people, guiding and directing them through the wilderness wanderings of Sinai, so the Son of God, Jesus, is with His people today through Word and Sacrament to forgive, nourish, preserve, guide, and direct us as we journey through the wilderness of life in this fallen world to the Promised Land of the new creation.

From Mount Sinai to the Promised Land (1:1–6:27)

The first six chapters of the book of Numbers detail God's preparation of His people at Mount Sinai. After taking a census of their tribes, making final preparations, and celebrating the Passover, they venture from the holy mountain toward the Promised Land.

A Census of Israel's Warriors (1:1–46)

 WAYPOINT

What strikes you most about this section as you read through it? Why?

The census was of only male warriors. How extensive do you suppose the full nation was, including men and women of all ages?

Amid prosperous times and times of want, how can God's people today keep the proper attitude of honoring and acknowledging God's provision and power in all things?

What does the specific role of the tribe of Levi show you about God's plan for the nation of His people?

What does this text show us?
God tells Moses and Aaron to take a census of His people, listing them by the names of their tribes. Men age 20 and older are counted, but not women and children. These men are the warriors God will use to drive the nations out of the Promised Land.

What does this text reveal about God's plan of salvation?
When Jacob and his family had left Canaan to travel to Egypt roughly four hundred years before, they were only seventy people in total. Now, God has increased this clan of people into a mighty nation with tribal divisions and an army. The promise God had made to Abraham—that he would be the father of a great nation—is now seen. As they set out from Mount Sinai, God prepares the warriors of this great nation to seize Canaan and thus receive the land He had promised to Abraham as well.

What does this text uncover about our identity and calling as God's people today?
Though the nation of Israel is mighty, their victory and power do not come from their own might but from the hand of God. The people so often forget this. In our own lives, God blesses us with varying degrees of prosperity at different times in life. Like the Israelites during this period, we are to find our source of security not in our own hands or in our own prosperity but in God's mercy and grace toward us.

Levites Exempted (1:47–54)

Of the twelve tribes of Israel, the Levites are excluded from the census. They will not fight in wars but will serve in the tabernacle and in other worship capacities.

VISUALIZE

The Camp Layout

Each time the people moved locations in the wilderness, the camp was taken down and set up following the same pattern. The tabernacle took a central place, and each tribe had a designated location for their tents.

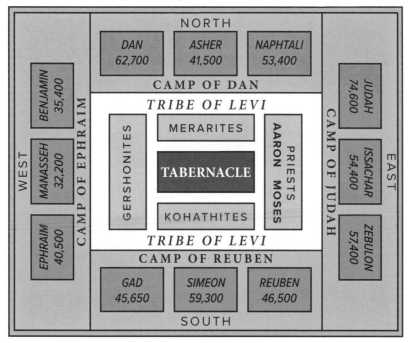

ARRANGEMENT OF THE CAMP (2:1–34)

God then arranges the way the Israelites will set up their tents as they travel toward the Promised Land. The tabernacle will be in the center of the camp, showing not only God's presence among them but also how they are to order their lives as His people.

What particular details about the arrangement of the camp stand out to you as you read this account? Why?

VISUALIZE

A Tent Home

Like many nomadic tribes, the Israelites lived in tents gathered in groups with other members of their extended family. Each tent had a fabric covering, with walls supported by wooden posts and anchored with ropes. Rugs and mats would have covered the ground, while pillows and cushions would be used for seating and sleeping. Cooking would be done outdoors beneath a fabric canopy that would protect from the sun and heat. The whole family would sleep together inside the tent. Nomadic people groups in the Middle East use similar tents today.

THE SONS OF AARON (3:1–4)

The names of Aaron's sons are listed. They and their descendants will serve as the family of high priests and priests for God's people.

DUTIES OF THE LEVITES (3:5–39)

God then assigns the clans of the tribe of Levi specific duties in guarding and transporting the many components of the tabernacle structure.

REDEMPTION OF THE FIRSTBORN (3:40–51)

According to God's Law, all the firstborn of Israel belong to God and should be removed from their tribes. In their place, however, God sets aside the entire tribe of Levi for the special worship duties of God's people.

DUTIES OF THE KOHATHITES (4:1–49)

Jacob's son Levi had three sons. The offspring of these sons formed the three clans of the Levites. All the Levite clans were to serve in guarding the tabernacle complex. One clan carried the tent walls and coverings and another carried the frames and bases over which the walls and

What stands out to you about the various work duties of the clans of the Levites?

What is the significance of God claiming the firstborn sons of the tribes of Israel within God's overall plan of salvation?

coverings were stretched. The clan of Kohath (Moses and Aaron's clan) had the special duty of carrying and maintaining the holy furnishings of the tabernacle, including the ark of the covenant, the incense altar, the lampstand, the bronze altar, and all the furnishings.

UNCLEAN PEOPLE (5:1–4)

God turns from instructions about the camp to a series of instructions about obeying His Law. He commands that anything ceremonially unclean must be put out of the camp because wherever the tabernacle stands is holy ground.

CONFESSION AND RESTITUTION (5:5–10)

Through Moses, God reminds His people that any sinful act done against anyone else is breaking God's Law. Offerings of repentance should be made when they sin.

A TEST FOR ADULTERY (5:11–31)

God then describes a lengthy and intricate process for determining the guilt or innocence of a woman who has been accused of committing adultery.

THE NAZIRITE VOW (6:1–21)

God gives a special regulation for His people. At certain times, individuals can take a special vow before God, voluntarily separating themselves for holy service to Him for a set time.

 VISUALIZE

A Nazirite

This icon of John the Baptist, with his long, uncut hair and untrimmed beard, depicts the classic image of someone who observes a Nazirite vow.

121

How might the specific aspects of the Nazirite vow have helped those who took it focus on holy service?

What was the purpose of the Nazirite vows?

Nazirite vows were a special declaration of faith that a Jew could make. One would pledge oneself to a greater-than-normal life of holiness that granted status equivalent to that of a Levite. It was primarily a vow of separation: abstinence from all grapevine products, cutting one's hair, and avoiding any contact with the dead. This vow didn't grant any special forgiveness or justification for the Jew who took it. Rather, it functioned similarly to the vow we make today in Confirmation. We make many other types of vows: marriage vows, citizenship vows, and vows we take when holding an office of special importance. The Nazirites show us that we should hold to our vows rigidly so that we may honor God, just as God faithfully keeps the vows He makes to His people.

Aaron's Blessing (6:22–27)

After the set of instructions about obeying God's Law, God gives Aaron a new threefold blessing to speak to His people. This Aaronic blessing, or benediction, has been repeated by God's people ever since, including in our worship services.

Consecrating the Tabernacle (7:1–12:16)

Offerings at the Tabernacle's Consecration (7:1–89)

Representatives of the twelve tribes present their various offerings at the tabernacle as a way to conclude the dedication. These offerings are identical for each tribe and given over a duration of twelve days.

The Seven Lamps (8:1–4)

There are no windows inside the tent of meeting, so God commands Aaron to light the menorah, a single golden lampstand designed to look like a tree. One lamp is in the middle, and three are on either side, designed to look like branches. These lamps are to illuminate the sacred space. This also represents how God's presence alone is their true light.

PICTURE OF THE SAVIOR

Seven Lamps

The tent of meeting in the tabernacle had no windows or any natural lighting features, and as a result of the heavy tent cloth, the interior often grew quite dark. God didn't overlook this detail, however. On Mount Sinai, He gave Moses the design for the menorah, the golden lampstand shaped like a tree, whose seven golden lamps chased away the darkness and allowed the priests to commune with Him. God was the only source of true light for the Israelites, and He remains the same for us too. His light, Jesus Christ, came to overcome the darkness of death for those who believe in Him. The lamps that illuminated the inside of the tent of meeting enabled believers to commune with God, just as Jesus enables us to come before the Father by His own gracious light.

LINK BETWEEN THE TESTAMENTS

The Seven Lamps (Numbers 8:1–4 → Revelation 4:2–5)

The menorah, the golden lampstand, stood in the Holy Place in the tabernacle, lighting up the room in front of the curtain that shielded the ark of the covenant, the dwelling place of God.

This arrangement resembled the heavenly throne room shown to us by John in Revelation 4: "At once I was in the Spirit, and behold, a throne stood in heaven, with one seated on the throne. . . . And before the throne were burning seven torches of fire, which are the seven spirits of God" (vv. 2, 5). Just as the seven lamps of the menorah shone out from the single lampstand, these seven torches represent the Holy Spirit, the Third Person of the Holy Trinity, who stands before God the Father on His throne and the Son of God, Jesus Christ, sitting at His right hand.

Cleansing of the Levites (8:5–22)

The Levites are then ceremonially cleansed for their service. From here on out, the Israelites will transfer their sins onto the Levites, who will then transfer those sins to animals to be sacrificed in the place of God's people.

Retirement of the Levites (8:23–26)

God establishes the retirement age of Levites from their service in the tabernacle at fifty years old.

In what ways does this ceremonial role of the Levites serve as a picture for what Jesus will do for God's people?

The Passover Celebrated (9:1–14)

God's people then celebrate the Passover before departing from Sinai, and God shows His mercy by allowing certain people to celebrate it at a different time because they were ceremonially unclean.

The Cloud Covering the Tabernacle (9:15–23)

God's presence in fire and cloud descends over the tabernacle as it is set up. From here on out, God's presence in the cloud will direct when and where His people will journey.

The Silver Trumpets (10:1–10)

God directs Moses to create two silver trumpets, which will be blown to signal both when the elders of Israel should gather and when Israel will break camp.

 VISUALIZE

Tabernacle Fixtures

This fragment from the Arch of Titus depicts Roman soldiers carrying off spoils from the temple in Jerusalem, including the silver trumpets and the menorah, also called the golden lampstand.

In what ways did God's presence in the cloud and the fire serve to form His people to fear, love, and trust in Him above all things?

ISRAEL LEAVES SINAI (10:11–36)

 WAYPOINT

What does this text show us?
Finally, after so much preparation and instruction from the Lord, the Israelites leave Mount Sinai and travel toward the Promised Land. God through Moses provides a detailed plan for operations, naming heads of tribes and marching orders. Through His presence in the cloud, God leads the way.

What does this text reveal about God's plan of salvation?
As the nation of God's people break camp, we see two distinct themes. On one hand, the traveling nation is going to be well-ordered and directed with Moses and the heads of tribes in positions of administrative leadership. On the other hand, it is God leading the way through the pillar of cloud, with the whole nation's movement focused around the ark of the covenant. God's people are given responsibilities in their various roles, but they are always called to follow God's lead. God's people today, called to faith in Jesus Christ through His means of grace, are also given different abilities and responsibilities. We, too, are called to follow where Jesus leads us through His Word, as the term *disciple*, meaning "follower," indicates.

What does this text uncover about our identity and calling as God's people today?
God provides His church with a variety of leaders and a variety of abilities. We are called to pray for and support those whom God has put in leadership and for each of us to serve as God has gifted us. Throughout it all, though, we are called to follow God's will through His Word as He leads His church to our eternal home.

How do you picture the scene of God's people breaking camp? What would it look like? What might it feel like to be part of it?

Where else in the Bible have you seen the cloud of God's glory or the ark of the covenant serving an important role in directing God's people?

How has God gifted you with talents and treasures? How can you use those to support and aid God's people as you follow God's lead through life?

THE PEOPLE COMPLAIN (11:1–15)

Shortly after they set out from Mount Sinai, God's people again complain about their food, especially their lack of meat. The anger of the Lord burns against them, and Moses pleads with God.

ELDERS APPOINTED TO AID MOSES (11:16–30)

God then appoints seventy men of the elders of the Israelites who will help Moses administer the duties of leadership. This was the establishment of the Jewish Council (known as the Sanhedrin, the Seventy), who would administer over Israel and eventually condemn Jesus to death. After their registration, the Spirit of the Lord descends on them.

What is significant about God giving the people quail as a punishment? How does this relate to how we frequently experience the consequences of our sins today?

QUAIL AND A PLAGUE (11:31–35)

God then sends the people a great number of quail to eat, but these bring with them a plague that strikes down many Israelites because their complaining stirred God's wrath.

MIRIAM AND AARON OPPOSE MOSES (12:1–16)

Even Moses' brother and sister join in opposing his leadership, and they must suffer the consequences of questioning God's authority. Their rebellion against God's appointed leader will encourage the other Israelites and Levites to question Moses' and Aaron's authority later on.

From the Promised Land to the Wilderness (13:1–14:45)

If you have heard that Israel wandered forty years in the wilderness, you may think that was God's plan for them all along. But chapters 13–21 show God's intention to settle His people in Canaan a little over a year from their exodus from Egypt. The events in these chapters explain why the wilderness wandering extended over the next forty years. During that time, God would refine the stubborn and rebellious Israelites into a mighty nation.

 VISUALIZE

From Sinai to the Promised Land

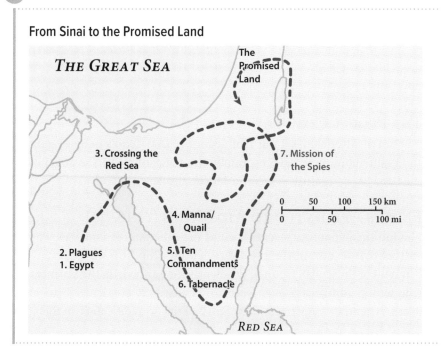

Spies Sent into Canaan (13:1–24)

Moses now sends twelve spies, one representative from each of the twelve tribes of Israel, into the Promised Land to gather information prior to their conquest.

Report of the Spies (13:25–33)

The spies return, and only two of the twelve, Joshua and Caleb, trust in God and give a positive report. The other ten forget God's power and are afraid of the inhabitants of the land. They discourage the people from believing they are strong enough to defeat the Canaanites.

What words or phrases from the reports of the ten faithless and two faithful spies stand out to you? Why?

The People Rebel (14:1–12)

The doubt and fear of the ten spies infect the Israelite camp, and the people begin to rebel against Moses and against God. They wish they would have died in Egypt or in the wilderness rather than dying against the Canaanites. They start looking for a leader to take them back to Egypt. God threatens to disinherit them, destroy them, and make a nation greater and mightier from Moses.

Moses Intercedes for the People (14:13–19)

Moses steps in and pleads with God not to destroy Israel, citing God's promises to His people. God relents out of His mercy.

Where else in the Bible do we see God's appointed leaders standing in and interceding before God for the sins of God's people?

God Promises Judgment (14:20–38)

Nevertheless, God promises that no man currently twenty years old or older will enter the Promised Land, except Joshua and Caleb. The people had seen God's great signs in Egypt and at the Red Sea but still did not trust in Him. Israel wishes they would have died in the wilderness, so God will grant their wish. They will spend the next forty years in the wilderness outside the Promised Land until the last of these men have fallen.

⊙ **WAYPOINT**

....

God's People Rebel and God Responds

What does this text show us?
In a powerful series of events, everything changes for God's people. Spies investigate Canaan, they bring back an unfavorable report, the seeds of a rebellion are born, God intends on destroying them, Moses intercedes, God relents, and God punishes the people. God's people are not ready to enter the Promised Land and will need to be refined for an entire generation.

What details of Numbers 13–14 are most surprising to you? Why?

What other connections do you see between what happened in Numbers 13–14 and what Jesus has done for us through His suffering, death, and resurrection?

What fears and insecurities tempt you the most to abandon your faith? How can you better turn those over to God in prayer?

What does this text reveal about God's plan of salvation?
In this tragic series of actions on behalf of God's people, and God's response, we see a picture of what Christ will do in fulfilling God's plan of salvation. Israel, terrified of the obstacles ahead, doubts God's faithfulness and turns against Moses. They wish they would have fallen in the wilderness. God, in His good judgment, justifiably seeks to bring His wrath against His rebellious people, but Moses, His anointed prophet, steps in and intercedes for the people, calling on God's mercy.

Likewise, humanity, in its sinful state, doubts God's Word and rebels against Him. In God's justice, we deserve nothing but His punishment both on earth and in eternity. Yet Jesus steps in, enacting God's mercy by dying on the cross in our place. God's people at the time of Moses have to suffer an earthly punishment for their sins: that generation will fall in the wilderness as they wished. Yet God is still faithful to provide their needs and bring their sons and daughters into the Promised Land. We in Christ, though we still must live in this broken world, will one day be brought to the greater promised land, the new creation, through the mercy and grace of Jesus.

What does this text uncover about our identity and calling as God's people today?
It's hard not to see ourselves reflected in the people of Israel here. After all, the fallen creation—the devil, the world, and our sinful flesh—constantly tempts us to reject God's promises or fight against His good will for us. Like the Israelites, however, we are without excuse before a good God. He is God and we are not. Christ interceded, however, to forgive us our sins. Despite our ongoing fears and temptations to reject God's Word and promise, God is faithful to us in Christ. As we travel through this world, looking to the promised land, may we find our identity as God's people solely in what He has done for us.

Israel Defeated in Battle (14:39–45)

When faced with forty years wandering, God's people change their plans and attempt to take the Promised Land by force without God's word. Disobeying God yet again, they are routed by their enemies and pursued out into the wilderness.

 VISUALIZE

The Promised Land

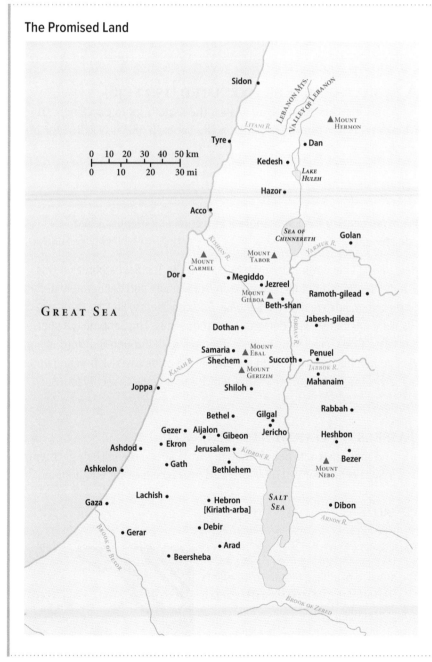

Religious Questions (15:1–19:22)

LAWS ABOUT SACRIFICES (15:1–21)

In a sign of His mercy and forgiveness, God offers instruction about how His people are to offer sacrifices when they take possession of the Promised Land once the forty years in the wilderness have passed.

LAWS ABOUT UNINTENTIONAL SINS (15:22–31)

God then reiterates laws about offering sacrifices for forgiveness of unintentional sins.

A SABBATHBREAKER EXECUTED (15:32–36)

Amid instruction on God's laws, the text shifts to describe a time when a man was found working on the Sabbath and was killed for his disobedience.

How do the words God speaks through Moses here demonstrate both His judgment and His mercy?

What are some consequences in our lives, both here and in eternity, when we neglect or despise listening to God's Word both in the congregation and on our own?

 CLEAR THE CONFUSION

Wasn't executing the Sabbathbreaker a cruel and inappropriate punishment?

Reread God's clear warning in Numbers 15:30–31. The Sabbathbreaker wasn't a well-intentioned but misguided man. He willfully and deliberately defied God's command to rest on the Sabbath. God considers willful disobedience of His Word an offense with damnable consequences. The Sabbath is a special day when God comes to us to strengthen our faith through His Word. When we intentionally ignore God on the day He set aside, we risk bringing upon ourselves the worst condemnation, which Jesus came to rectify for us.

TASSELS ON GARMENTS (15:37–41)

God then instructs people to make and use tassels on their garments as a visual reminder of His Word and presence among His people.

 VISUALIZE

Tassels

The practice of adding tassels to garments as a reminder of God's Word and presence is still practiced today. This prayer shawl is typical of those used by Jewish people throughout history.

Korah's Rebellion (16:1–50)

 WAYPOINT

What does this text show us?

Korah, a Levite, leads an insurrection against Moses and Aaron's position as Israel's leaders. He persuades 250 prominent chiefs and Levites to join him. Through Moses, God commands Aaron and the chiefs to bring censers with fire and incense to present before the tent of meeting. The glory of the Lord appears, and He threatens once again to destroy the entire nation, but again Moses intercedes. Moses tells the congregation to separate themselves from the rebels. God causes the ground to open up and swallow Korah's group, and fire from heaven strikes down the chiefs with their censers. The next day, the people grumble against Moses for killing the chiefs, and God sends a plague that kills many Israelites until Aaron offers incense on his altar and it is stopped.

What does this text reveal about God's plan of salvation?

This is a challenging narrative for many, especially considering the sheer amount of death that comes to Israel because of their sins. Not only the Levite Korah but also his followers, their families, and so many others die because they challenge Moses' authority. It is important first to consider the honor God had given to Korah and all of these chiefs. Korah was Moses and Aaron's first cousin, a member of the clan of Kohath, which was honored to care for the holy furnishings of the tabernacle. But Korah, his fellow Levites, and the chiefs of Israel were not content with the great honor God had given them. These were prominent and influential leaders who were leading the Israelites against God.

This scene of Dathan and Abiram and their families being swallowed up by the earth is a vivid picture of hell and a warning against rejecting God and His authority. Here we see just how important the roles of God's anointed are to Him. God set aside Moses and Aaron for a special purpose, and challenging their authority was directly challenging God and His authority. This points us to Christ, the final Anointed One, whom God set aside for a special purpose to do His work of redeeming the world. A challenge against Christ is a challenge against God but in a much greater sense than it was with Moses, as the Christ is God Himself.

What does this text uncover about our identity and calling as God's people today?

This narrative shows us that God takes His authority seriously. This serves as a warning for all, including Christians, of God's power and how He cannot be challenged. It is only by His grace, as poured out on us in Jesus Christ, that we can stand before Him. We praise God for the gift of Christ, who stands before

 What does this narrative show us about the nature of holy things and how God wants us to treat that which is holy?

 In what other ways does this section prefigure the final judgment?

In what ways do people today dishonor God or disrespect His authority? What habits can you form that will help you avoid following those thoughts or behaviors?

131

the throne of God the Father and intercedes for us. Through Him, we have redemption, forgiveness of sins, and rescue from the final judgment. As we go through life, confident in our salvation, we are called to take God, His Word, and His command seriously, as He alone is the first and final authority in the universe.

What does the fact that God provided a miracle to prove Aaron's headship among the priests show us about who God is?

AARON'S STAFF BUDS (17:1–13)

To establish His choice of Aaron and his sons once and for all, God gathers a leader from each tribe and commands each one to bring a staff to set before the tent of meeting. In one night, God makes Aaron's staff sprout, bud, and produce ripe almonds.

DUTIES OF PRIESTS AND LEVITES (18:1–32)

Having confirmed His choice of Aaron, God shows His forgiveness and grace as He now reaffirms the role of the Levites to serve Aaron. Though many Levites had joined in Korah's rebellion, God forgives them and reestablishes their important work for Israel.

LAWS FOR PURIFICATION (19:1–22)

God then gives instructions on how those who have come in contact with dead bodies can become ceremonially clean again. Only those who are clean or have been cleansed can come near His presence in the tabernacle.

Journey Back toward the Promised Land (20:1–21:35)

THE DEATH OF MIRIAM (20:1)

The forty years have now passed, and God directs His people once again toward the Promised Land. Miriam, Moses and Aaron's sister, dies.

THE WATERS OF MERIBAH (20:2–9)

Passing through a region with no water, the people once again grumble against God and Moses. God tells Moses to take the staff, assemble the congregation, and speak to the rock to bring forth water for them. God is gracious to them, despite their rebellious, unbelieving hearts.

MOSES STRIKES THE ROCK (20:10–13)

 **WAYPOINT**

What does this text show us?

God commands Moses to speak to a rock to provide water for God's whining people. In his impulsive anger, Moses adds to God's command and strikes the rock rather than speaking God's command. Water does come from the rock to God's people, but as a consequence of Moses' action, God tells Moses he will not be allowed to enter the Promised Land.

What does this text reveal about God's plan of salvation?

A vital need of the people is water, and God has given it to them in various ways and at various times. Moses is commanded to speak to a rock but disobeys God by striking the rock. The picture this paints is powerful. Around forty years earlier, God had provided water for His people in a similar way (Exodus 17:6). At that time, God had said He would stand before them on a rock, and when Moses struck the rock, water would pour fourth from it. This evokes an image of God being struck and providing water and nourishment for His people from that wound. In this instance, Moses is asked simply to speak to a rock so that water would come forth, but in what is likely a lack of trust, he strikes the rock again. Even so, God gives the people water. When Jesus died on the cross, He demonstrated not only God's patience and grace toward His sinful people but also how God continues to pour out His forgiveness. Jesus' side was pierced and water flowed out, hearkening back to these events in the wilderness.

What does this text uncover about our identity and calling as God's people today?

Like Moses, we are called upon to follow God's commandments, even when we do not understand them or doubt God's reasoning. Even though there are earthly consequences for our acts of disobedience, we can, like Moses, trust that our eternal futures are assured by Christ.

 How are the complaints of the people similar to and different from their complaints elsewhere during the time of wilderness wanderings?

 What does God's rebuke to Moses show about the responsibilities God gives to leaders in the church?

 How can times when we experience the earthly consequences for our sinful actions serve as times of growth and learning for us?

 **CLEAR THE CONFUSION**

Why did God disqualify Moses from leading Israel into the Promised Land for something so small?

Moses disobeyed God when he struck the rock instead of only speaking to it to draw out the water God promised would be there. As God's representative to the people, Moses was portraying God as angry and grudging toward His people instead of gracious, patient, merciful, and loving. Instead of building

133

trust in Israel toward God, Moses was giving the impression that God would act on their behalf only out of anger. Moses showed unfaithfulness to God, and such unfaithfulness had consequences. This account helps us to remember that even the greatest heroes of faith stumbled due to their sinful nature and that all mankind is in need of a Savior to save us from our sins.

What are some important details about this interaction that stand out to you? Why?

EDOM REFUSES PASSAGE (20:14–21)

Instead of entering the Promised Land from Kadesh-barnea in the south, God will lead His people across the Jordan River in the east. Along the way, Moses implores the Edomites, descendants of Jacob's brother, Esau, to allow the Israelites passage through their territory to the Promised Land, promising to pay for any water they or their livestock drink. The Edomites refuse them passage.

What do we learn from this text about the nature of the priestly office?

THE DEATH OF AARON (20:22–29)

God announces that the time has come for Aaron the high priest to die. Moses leads Aaron and Eleazar, his son, up Mount Hor. Moses strips Aaron of his priestly garments and dresses the next generation. The mortality of Aaron's line of high priests stands out throughout the Old Testament. Jesus, our great High Priest, dies on the cross but rises again to be our eternal High Priest sitting at the Father's right hand in heaven.

ARAD DESTROYED (21:1–3)

Seeing the Israelites approaching the Promised Land, the Canaanite king of neighboring Arad attacks and takes some of them captive. The Israelites obediently come to God for guidance, and He gives the armies and cities of Arad to the Israelites to be completely destroyed. Through these victories on the way to the Promised Land, Israel is learning to trust God and be confident in His promises.

The Bronze Serpent (21:4–9)

WAYPOINT

What does this text show us?

God's people again grumble against Him, and God sends venomous serpents into the camp. When the people cry out, God instructs Moses to make a bronze serpent on a pole and place it in the middle of the camp. Whoever looks at it, trusting God's promise, is saved.

What does this text reveal about God's plan of salvation?

This short episode encapsulates the main themes of God's plan of salvation. God chooses a people, who then rebel, suffer the consequences of their rebellion, cry out for help, and are saved by God's mercy and grace. Even the appearance of serpents in this narrative reminds us of Satan in the Garden of Eden, and the command to put a bronze serpent on a pole reminds us of God's promise that an offspring of Eve would crush Satan's power.

What does this text uncover about our identity and calling as God's people today?

Just as God's people in the wilderness could receive rescue only from their self-inflicted punishment by trusting God's promise as they looked at the bronze serpent, God's people today only find forgiveness and salvation in the cross of Christ. Christ was lifted up on that cross, and we look to Him for our salvation. This is our Christian identity as God's rebellious yet redeemed people, and we are called to keep our eyes focused on the cross of Christ as we journey though the daily life of faith.

What are some details that stick out to you from this narrative? What do they show you about what the people were like and what God is like?

How does this section show us the nature of repentance and forgiveness?

Looking at physical crosses throughout your day can be a powerful reminder of what Christ has done for you. Where can you place a cross or multiple crosses in your home or workspace to help remind you of your identity in Christ?

PICTURE OF THE SAVIOR

Bronze Serpent

It seemed as though the Israelites could not get any worse. God's people had failed to believe in Him again and again since Mount Sinai, disobeying and rebelling against Him at every turn. Aaron and Miriam had died, a whole generation was condemned to death in the desert, and even Moses was barred from leading the Israelites into the Promised Land. Yet even here, at one of their lowest points, God had mercy upon His people as He taught them. Moses went to God in repentant prayer to ask for a solution to the punishment of fiery serpents, and God answered him with a task: raise a bronze (fiery) serpent on a pole, and those who look upon it would live. The serpent itself did not possess magic healing powers of any kind, for it was the faith in God's promise that healed the bitten Israelite people. In this same way, Jesus was lifted up on a cross so that we might see Him, believe in Him, and live eternally on account of what He has done. For as Jesus Himself said to Nicodemus, "As Moses lifted up the serpent in the wilderness, so must the Son of Man be lifted up, that whoever believes in Him may have eternal life" (John 3:14–15).

What stands out to you from this text about how God had formed His people in their wilderness experiences?

The Song of the Well (21:10–20)

As the Israelites close in on the Promised Land, on the east side of the Jordan River, do you notice anything different about God's people? Instead of griping and complaining about their thirst, they wait patiently for God, trusting He will provide in His time. God speaks first: "Gather the people together, so that I may give them water" (v. 16). When He does, the Israelites sing songs of joy.

King Sihon Defeated (21:21–30)

Like the Edomites before them, the Amorites deny the Israelites passage through their territory to the Promised Land. Sihon, one Amorite king, assembles his army to attack the Israelites, his army is defeated, and God gives his land to Israel. This territory will form the easternmost regions where God's people will settle.

Picture in your mind what it would have been like to witness the defeats of Sihon and Og. What would it have been like as an Israelite during this time?

King Og Defeated (21:31–35)

Following suit, another Amorite king, Og, goes to war against Israel. We read an interesting statement from God to Moses: "Do not fear him, for I have given him into your hand" (v. 34). This makes sense when Moses recalls this event in the first of his farewell sermons to Israel. In Deuteronomy 3:11, Moses tell us Og is a giant, but Og is powerless to stand against Israel's God. His territory will also become settlements for the Israelites east of the Jordan River. These victories over two powerful kings reassure Israel that they can trust God to give them victory over the Canaanites.

 CLEAR THE CONFUSION

Many times in the Psalms, we read about Sihon and Og. Why are the defeats of kings Sihon and Og such a big deal?

When the Israelites defeated these kings, they conquered the last people that stood in their path to the Promised Land. These victories gave them access to the land east of the Jordan, which God had promised to them. But even more importantly, these victories gave the children of Israel a confidence in God that their fathers had lacked at Kadesh-barnea. They could trust God to faithfully keep His promise to give them the land of Canaan. Only with God was Israel able to do what many would have considered impossible.

Preparing to Enter the Promised Land (22:1–25:18)

Chapters 22–36 detail events that happen immediately before God's people cross the Jordan River into the Promised Land. This includes opposition by Balak, a new census, the giving of new laws, the defeat of Midian, and final preparations.

BALAK SUMMONS BALAAM (22:1–21)

After witnessing the defeat of the Amorites, King Balak of the Moabites summons the mysterious soothsayer Balaam to curse the Israelites. Balak believes that Balaam has power over the Lord. God commands Balaam not to go to Balak, but greedy Balaam, seeking personal gain, ignores God's warning.

What does this text reveal to you about the perspective and attitude of those people living in Canaan who witnessed God's people preparing for conquest?

BALAAM'S DONKEY AND THE ANGEL (22:22–41)

⊙ WAYPOINT

What does this text show us?
God teaches Balaam a lesson in listening to Him. Since Balaam has already refused to obey God, the Angel of the Lord appears before Balaam, and God makes Balaam's donkey talk. At God's warning, Balaam refuses to offer any curse for Balak against the Israelites that goes against God's Word.

What does this text reveal about God's plan of salvation?
At first glance, the idea of a talking donkey seems ludicrous. Yet God allowing the animal to talk illustrates an important point: the beast understands better than the soothsayer Balaam how foolish it is to go against God. When the Angel of the Lord, likely the preincarnate Christ, stands in Balaam's path to keep him from speaking curses against God's people, Balaam has no option. When Balaam's eyes are open to see what the donkey sees, he cannot but confess his sins and obey God's commands. The Angel of the Lord directs the course of God's plan of salvation, working both in the forefront and behind the scenes to bring God's people to the Promised Land. Just like the donkey would speak the truth, God would then use the unbelieving Balaam to speak the truth of God's blessings to Balak and all of Moab.

What strikes you most about how God deals with Balaam here, and why?

Where else in the Bible do we seen the Angel of the Lord directly intervening to direct God's plan of salvation?

What are some bad habits that you've gotten into that lead you to think that God doesn't know or care about your sins? How can you work to break those habits and take God's Word more seriously in your daily life?

What does this text uncover about our identity and calling as God's people today?

Like Balaam, our foolish pride and sense of self-importance can make us feel like we can get away with sins despite God's warning. We have received God's Word and Commandments, in which God makes it clear what we are to think, say, and do in our daily lives. Even so, in our sin, we think that somehow God doesn't notice or care if certain things slide. This narrative serves as a reminder to us of just how foolish this attitude is. God knows and cares. The Angel of the Lord, the Son of God, cares so much that He came to earth to bear the very punishments that you and I and Balaam deserve for our sins. As God's forgiven children, then, we take His commands seriously and check our attitudes against pride, complacency, and thinking that somehow God doesn't care about small-scale sins.

BALAAM'S FIRST ORACLE (23:1–12)

Whereas Balak desires a curse, Balaam instead offers a blessing to the Israelites on the border of the Promised Land.

What particular words or phrases from these oracles stand out to you? Why?

BALAAM'S SECOND ORACLE (23:13–30)

Bringing Balaam to a new location, Balak hopes that the soothsayer will try again and curse the Israelites. Instead, Balaam again offers a blessing to the Israelites.

BALAAM'S THIRD ORACLE (24:1–14)

Unable to curse the Israelites, Balaam offers up a third blessing for them, praising Israel and reiterating God's promises to them.

What words or phrases from this final oracle specifically point us to Jesus? How did Jesus fulfill these prophecies about Him?

BALAAM'S FINAL ORACLE (24:15–25)

Balaam then offers up a final blessing, this time pointing to a future event: the coming Messiah, who would one day rise out of Jacob.

CLEAR THE CONFUSION

Why is Balaam significant?

Balaam teaches us the importance of humility and deference before God. Balaam was greedy and thought that he could twist the will of God and the machinations of Balak to his own monetary gain, but God humbled him and made him see that he could not control God or use Him to achieve his own perverse ends. We should be wary of the same sentiments in ourselves and seek God as our almighty Father, not a divine pawn that we can manipulate. Thankfully, God used a reluctant Balaam to prophesy about Jesus Christ, who would come to atone for this kind of sinful arrogance and redeem those who have been lost to greed and other worldly desires.

BAAL WORSHIP AT PEOR (25:1–9)

Balaam is unable to satisfy Balak or receive money when God forbids him to put a curse on Israel. But Balaam is unwilling to leave that reward aside, so he wickedly plots to cause the Israelites to bring a curse upon themselves. He counsels the Moabites to invite the men of Israel to join them in the wicked pagan fertility rituals of the people of Moab (see Numbers 31:16). We see the extent of the disobedience when God commands Moses to hang all the chiefs of the people lest all Israel follow the example of these faithless leaders. God also sends a plague that kills twenty-four thousand.

Where else in the Bible do we see God's people being tempted in a similar way? How are we tempted to disobey God's will in a similar way today?

The faithful Israelites join Moses before the tent of meeting, weeping in repentance when they see an Israelite man defiantly leading a Moabite woman into his tent. In holy zeal, Aaron's grandson Phinehas kills both of them, stopping God's anger.

THE ZEAL OF PHINEHAS (25:10–18)

God commends Phinehas for his zeal and reconfirms the role of Aaron's descendants as priests.

The Second Census and New Laws (26:1–27:23)

 VISUALIZE

Taking the Census

Taking the census would have required a variety of tools to record and tabulate the numbers reported by each tribe of Israel. Ancient records were often kept on an early form of paper called papyrus or on clay tablets incised with patterns.

CENSUS OF THE NEW GENERATION (26:1–65)

 **WAYPOINT**

What does this text show us?
As was done and recorded in the first chapter of Numbers, Moses takes another census of the warriors of Israel. This is a numbering of the new generation, the grown children of the exodus, since the previous generation, except Joshua and Caleb, has died in the wilderness because of their unfaithfulness at Kadesh-barnea.

What does this text reveal about God's plan of salvation?
Now that the time of wilderness wanderings is complete, God's people prepare to enter the Promised Land. This section includes a description of how the land would be divided up among the tribes. In God's plan of salvation, after forty years of waiting and being refined, God's people are ready to enter the land under their new leader, Joshua. God's promises would come to pass and the people would dwell in their land, waiting for the coming of the Messiah.

What does this text uncover about our identity and calling as God's people today?
When you look back at your life, the good and bad times, you can see the ways circumstances and experiences have shaped you into the person you are today. In Christ, we have the assurance that no matter what we've done or experienced, God is faithful and just to forgive us as we confess our sins. Regardless of what you've been through, God is able to use those experiences to help you love and serve your neighbor. Just like He did with His people in

What details from this section show just how much God had prepared and refined His people during their wilderness wanderings?

How has God worked through challenging times in your life to form you for greater love and service to your neighbor?

the wilderness, God continues to form your faith and life for service to your neighbor through His Word and your daily struggles in this fallen creation.

THE DAUGHTERS OF ZELOPHEHAD (27:1–11)

A group of sisters, whose father had died in the wilderness without any sons, pleads with Moses in order to inherit their father's possessions. God makes a provision for inheritance to be passed on to a man's daughters if he dies with no sons.

JOSHUA TO SUCCEED MOSES (27:12–23)

As the time of Moses' death draws near, God appoints Joshua, one of the two faithful spies from the previous generation, as the new leader of His people.

How does this section reveal to us God's justice and mercy?

 LINK BETWEEN THE TESTAMENTS

Commissioning of Joshua → Commissioning of Peter
(Numbers 27 → John 21)

Moses was drawing near to the end of his time leading God's people, and he needed someone who could step up and bring Israel into the Promised Land. God provided him with Joshua, one "in whom is the Spirit" (v. 18), to take his mantle into a land where he could not go. Moses laid his hands upon Joshua before the people and imparted to him the authority that God had given him for his task. Now, fast-forward to the very end of Jesus' ministry on earth. A remarkably similar scene unfolds after a final breakfast between the Son of God and Peter, who had shunned Him the night of His crucifixion. After Peter affirms his love for Jesus three times, Jesus charges him, saying, "Feed My sheep. Truly, truly, I say to you, when you were young, you used to dress yourself and walk wherever you wanted, but when you are old, you will stretch out your hands, and another will dress you and carry you where you do not want to go" (John 21:17–18). In just the three words at the beginning, Jesus reinstates Peter as His disciple. He then declares that Peter would lead His church on earth until his martyrdom before the Roman emperor. God calls leaders of His church to pass down the mantle of guidance and direction as time passes and continually provides for us in providential transitions like these.

God Confirms Offering Practices (28:1–30:16)

DAILY OFFERINGS (28:1–8)

God instructs the new generation, on the border of the Promised Land, on offerings they are to faithfully bring Him.

?

As you read over the offering practices in the following chapters, consider how these are similar to and different from offerings that Christians give to the service of the church.

◉ VISUALIZE

VARIOUS OFFERINGS	
Sabbath	Two male lambs, each a year old, grain offering, drink offering
Monthly	Two bulls, one ram, seven male lambs, grain offering, wine
Passover	Two bulls, one ram, seven male lambs, flour/oil, drink offering; offered throughout the week
Feast of Weeks	Two bulls, one ram, seven male lambs, flour/oil, drink offering; offered throughout the week
Feast of Trumpets	Two bulls, one ram, seven male lambs, flour/oil, drink offering; offered throughout the week
Day of Atonement	Two bulls, one ram, seven male lambs, one male goat, flour/oil, drink offering
FEAST OF BOOTHS	
Day 1	Thirteen bulls, two rams, fourteen male lambs, one male goat, grain offering
Day 2	Twelve bulls, two rams, fourteen male lambs, one male goat, grain offering
Day 3	Eleven bulls, two rams, fourteen male lambs, one male goat, grain offering
Day 4	Ten bulls, two rams, fourteen male lambs, one male goat, grain offering
Day 5	Nine bulls, two rams, fourteen male lambs, one male goat, grain offering
Day 6	Eight bulls, two rams, fourteen male lambs, one male goat, grain offering
Day 7	Seven bulls, two rams, fourteen male lambs, one male goat, grain offering
Day 8	One bull, one ram, seven male lambs, one male goat, grain offering.

Sabbath Offerings (28:9–10)

Likewise, God instructs His people on weekly Sabbath offerings.

Monthly Offerings (28:11–15)

God restates His desires for Israel's monthly offerings.

Passover Offerings (28:16–25)

God now turns to instructing His people on proper offering and worship practices for the yearly festivals, starting with the offerings to be made in the central festival of Passover at the beginning of the Israelite year. This festival recalls God delivering His people from slavery in Egypt.

Offerings for the Feast of Weeks (28:26–31)

God gives instruction on another major yearly festival, the Feast of Weeks, which would later be known as Pentecost. This festival is related to thanking God for the harvest.

Offerings for the Feast of Trumpets (29:1–6)

God reiterates His instruction on offerings for the Feast of Trumpets. The blasting of the trumpets on this holy day of celebration would remind the people that God is their King.

Offerings for the Day of Atonement (29:7–11)

Offering practices are described for the Day of Atonement, a festival day each year when God's people were especially called to repentance and faith, recalling God's undeserved mercy to them and pointing ahead to Good Friday, the day Jesus Christ atoned for the sins of the world.

Offerings for the Feast of Booths (29:12–40)

Finally, God gives special instruction for offering sacrifices during the Feast of Booths. This festival time is to be celebrated to recall God's faithfulness to His people in bringing them through the wilderness to the Promised Land.

Men and Vows (30:1–2)

God emphasized the severity of what happens when a man makes a vow in God's name and does not keep it.

Women and Vows (30:3–16)

Special care is then given to tell how women are to keep their vows. This highlights the role of women as dependents in this context and also shows the interconnected nature of being trustworthy in our communities.

What are some of the benefits for Christians today, just like the Israelites in the Old Testament, of keeping a yearly schedule of religious worship, celebration, and remembrance?

The Defeat of Midian (31:1–32:42)

What do the details of this text reveal to you about the nature of the conquest of the Promised Land?

How does this text show us another glimpse of the faith God worked in this second generation?

VENGEANCE ON MIDIAN (31:1–54)

God now gives Moses a final task, to oversee the complete destruction of the Midianites, who had previously tempted His people into idolatry. Phinehas will oversee the operations and through this conquest will secure territory to the east of the Jordan River for God's people. Notice that Balaam was killed in this war (v. 8).

REUBEN AND GAD SETTLE IN GILEAD (32:1–42)

After the successful military conquest of the land east of the Jordan, the tribes of Reuben and Gad desire to settle there. At first, Moses fears these two tribes are repeating the sin at Kadesh-barnea, when the first generation of Israel refused to go into the Promised Land. But when the tribes of Reuben and Gad promise to lead their brothers into the Promised Land to capture it, God agrees.

 CLEAR THE CONFUSION

What led these tribes to settle in the Trans-Jordan area?

The tribes of Reuben and Gad were rich in livestock and saw that the land east of the Jordan River in Gilead and Jazer was profitable for raising their herds. They beseeched Moses, asking him to allow them to remain in these lands. The tribes of Reuben and Gad offered to assist their brothers in the conquest of the land. Moses agreed on this condition, reminding them that their promise was one made to God, and so the tribes of Reuben and of Gad and half the tribe of Manasseh were granted the land Israel had taken from the Amorites, east of the Jordan River.

The Final Preparations (33:1–36:13)

What specific details does Moses choose to dwell on more than others, and how might that be significant?

RECOUNTING ISRAEL'S JOURNEY (33:1–49)

Moses, the author of the book of Numbers, then recalls in great detail each step of the journey of God's people from slavery in Egypt to their current place on the banks of the Jordan River. This travelogue would remind Israel of how God faithfully protected and provided for them in the inhospitable wilderness.

Drive Out the Inhabitants (33:50–56)

God commands His people to completely drive out the inhabitants of Canaan from the land and to destroy all idols when they go in to conquer it. His primary concern is not allow the false religions of the Canaanites to influence or tempt God's people away from true worship, as the Midianites had previously done. Israel's failure to obey this command would lead to great heartache throughout the rest of the Old Testament history of Israel.

Boundaries of the Land (34:1–15)

Through Moses, God then sets the specific boundaries for the Promised Land, which they are to conquer. He then commands that the specific tribes will determine their boundaries within the Promised Land by lot, taking into account the tribes already established east of the Jordan. Joshua and Eleazar the priest, Aaron's grandson, divide this land in Joshua 15–19.

What do these God-given boundaries reveal to you about the nature of this war?

List of Tribal Chiefs (34:16–29)

God then establishes the names of the tribal chiefs who will be in charge of dividing the land once it is conquered.

Cities for the Levites (35:1–8)

Levi was the one tribe that inherited no land in Israel. Jacob (Israel) had foretold this in his final words to his twelve sons. This prophecy, spoken in Genesis 49:5–7, was based on Levi joining with Simeon to murder the men of Shechem after their sister, Dinah, had been raped: "I will divide them in Jacob and scatter them in Israel." God sets aside forty-eight cities throughout the tribal lands of the Israelites in which the Levites can teach the faith to their Israelite brothers.

From the text, what do you suppose it would have been like to live in one of these Levite cities? How would it be similar to and different from living in other Israelite cities?

Cities of Refuge (35:9–34)

Six of the cities of the Levites will also serve as cities of refuge, where those guilty of accidental manslaughter can flee to avoid revenge killing. Note that these cities of refuge are not to harbor intentional murderers. When the anointed high priest died, all those guilty of accidental manslaughter were free to return to their dwelling places without fear of vengeance. This pointed ahead to Jesus Christ, our great High Priest. By His death, we are free of God's vengeance and wrath for our sins.

VISUALIZE

Cities of Refuge

God established six cities of refuge (marked in red on the map). These cities were run by the Levites and provided a safe space for those who had unintentionally committed manslaughter.

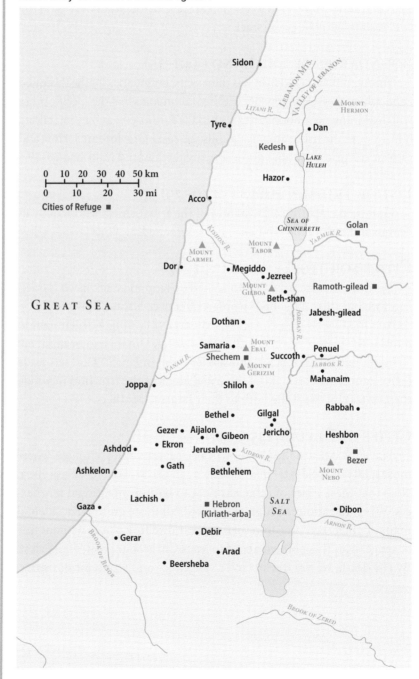

PICTURE OF THE SAVIOR

City of Refuge

In a time marked by blood feuds, grudges, and revenge killings on behalf of family, God established a legal process by which the matter of judging and punishing might be solved in a way that pointed ahead to Jesus Christ. An ancient custom allowed the deceased's next of kin to avenge the life of his or her family and, as a result, this system did not allow for the sanctity of life and justice to flourish. Moses was charged to work with the Israelites to create six cities of refuge in the Promised Land—three in Canaan and three beyond the Jordan River—to which people who had accidentally killed someone else could flee for protection. In these cities, the accused would be protected and properly judged according to the counsel of each city's elders. As long as the high priest at the time of the crime was alive, the accused had to live in that city, for the high priest's life itself was seen as atonement for the sin of the accused, and no harm would come to him or her on that account. Once the high priest died, the accused was freed to return to his or her own land. In our condition of original sin, we are condemned to death by the Law and can flee only to Jesus Christ, who is our city of refuge. We receive the grace of justification when we live in Him by the Holy Spirit. Unlike the high priests, however, Jesus has conquered death and lives forevermore. We can stay with Him eternally in His tender mercy and care, freed from the shackles of sin, death, and the devil.

Marriage of Female Heirs (36:1–13)

In chapter 27, Zelophehad's daughters were promised the land their father left behind since he had not had any sons. The heads of that clan recognized a potential problem. If the daughters of Zelophehad were to marry outside their tribe, their father's land would transfer to the tribe of their husband. God protects tribal inheritance by establishing that in such circumstances when daughters inherit their father's land, they must marry within their own tribes. That prevented land inheritance from being passed between tribes.

The book of Numbers ends with this discussion about land inherited in Israel, God's assurance that He will bring His people across the Jordan to give them the inheritance He had promised to their forefathers Abraham, Isaac, and Jacob.

DEUTERONOMY

Welcome to Deuteronomy

The name *Deuteronomy* means literally "second law" and reflects how Moses uses this opportunity to reteach God's laws to His people. He encourages the nation to continue to trust God as He prepares to lead them into the Promised Land.

In his fifth book, Moses reminds the Israelites of God's laws given at Sinai. Facing the punishment for their unfaithfulness, the people need the reminder of God's continuing grace and mercy. Moses summarizes much of the content from the book of Exodus, written as a narrative.

At the time the book of Deuteronomy is written, most of the older generation that had escaped from Egypt has died during the forty years in the wilderness. Now Moses wants to remind the second generation of the events of these years past and how God has been with them throughout this time of wandering. As you marvel at God's presence among His people through the difficult years in the wilderness, remember that He is with you always, guiding you to your eternal home with Him.

What do you know about Deuteronomy already? What would you like to learn about this book? What do you expect to get out of it by reading it?

Deuteronomy at a Glance

- **Start:** Deuteronomy begins near the end of Israel's forty years of wandering in the wilderness.

- **End:** Deuteronomy ends with the death of Moses as the people prepare to enter the Promised Land.

- **Theme:** God renews His covenant with the children of Israel as they prepare to enter the Promised Land.

- **Author and Date:** The final book of the prophet Moses was likely written around 1407–1406 BC.

- **Places Visited:** The plains of Moab, Mount Ebal, Mount Nebo

- **Journey Time:** The thirty-four chapters of Deuteronomy can be read in two and a half hours.

- **Outline:**
  - Historical Prologue (1:1–4:43)
  - Reviewing the Covenant (4:44–23:14)
  - Miscellaneous Laws (23:15–28:68)
  - Renewing the Covenant (29:1–30:20)
  - Leadership Succession (31:1–34:12)

Five Top Sights and Spectacles of Deuteronomy

God Gives His People Victory (2:26–3:22) Observe the consequences for King Sihon and King Og when they ignore the request of the Israelites to pass peacefully through their territories.

God Gives His Commandments on Sinai (5:1–6:25) Listen as Moses recalls the giving of the Law on Mount Sinai.

At Mount Ebal (27:1–28:68) Watch as the Israelites gather for worship as they prepare to enter the Promised Land.

God Renews the Covenant (29:1–30:20) Learn about how God renews His covenant promise with His chosen people.

God Prepares the Transfer of Leadership (31:1–34:12) Witness how God prepares Moses and Aaron for the change in leadership as the people wrap up their time in the wilderness.

Seeing Jesus in Deuteronomy

In the book of Deuteronomy, Moses serves to prefigure the coming of Jesus Christ, the one who would bring His people out of the land of slavery to sin into the promised land of eternal life with Him. The Old Testament high priest prefigured Jesus, our High Priest, who would make the perfect and final sacrifice for our sins. Moses says, "The Lord your God will raise up for you a prophet like me from among you, from your brothers—it is to Him you shall listen" (18:15).

Historical Prologue (1:1–4:43)

After forty years of wandering in the wilderness. Israel is camped on the east bank of the Jordan River looking across at the Promised Land. Moses preaches a series of farewell sermons, starting with a reminder of Israel's last forty years, which began at Mount Sinai.

THE COMMAND TO LEAVE HOREB (1:1–8)

After the Israelites received the Ten Commandments and built the tabernacle according to God's instructions, God directed them to move toward the land first promised to Abraham to take possession of it.

 CLEAR THE CONFUSION

Why mention the specific eleven-day journey from Mount Seir to Kadesh-barnea?

Moses mentioned this specific leg of the journey (1:2) to indicate that Kadesh-barnea was the gateway through which Israel would have entered and possessed the Promised Land. Their journey seemed to be complete but, beginning with the bad report of most of the spies, Israel's unfaithfulness sentenced them to thirty-eight more years of wandering in the desert. By highlighting this in a place where the land is once again open before Israel, Moses alludes to the fact that, like them, their fathers were extremely close and still managed to turn away from God's gift. Inasmuch as this was a warning for the Israelites, let Moses' words also caution us from unfaithfulness to God.

 WAYPOINT

Moses' First Message (1:6–4:43)

What does this text show us?
Moses recounts the history of the children of Israel from their captivity and slavery in Egypt to present time. These summaries were designed to cause the Israelites to recall God's continued care throughout their time in the wilderness.

What does this text reveal about God's plan of salvation?
God gave the Israelites His prophet Moses to lead and guide His people to the Promised Land first made known to their father Abraham. Moses foreshadows the One who would come to bring all believers to spend eternity with their Creator in the new heaven and new earth.

What does this text uncover about our identity and calling as God's people today?
The children of Israel pass through the waters of the Red Sea as God leads them through on dry ground. God has made us His own people through the waters of Baptism.

We often have to wait for things we desire. How do you suppose the Israelites felt when they heard that it was finally time to leave the wilderness?

After reading through these chapters, skim through again to look for significant events in the lives of the Israelites.

God revealed His direction for His people through the life and work of Moses. How did He continue to guide and direct His people throughout the Scriptures?

Consider all the promises God has made to you. How has He kept all of these promises?

LEADERS APPOINTED (1:9–18)

Moses tells how he needed assistance in dealing with the growing population of the Israelites. Moses selected leaders from each of the tribes to assist in the work.

 SET THE SCENE

The LORD Your God

The phrase "the LORD your God" occurs around 250 times in the book of Deuteronomy. Through this repeated name for God, the people were reminded of how He brought them out of Egypt and continued to be with them.

Why did the Israelites find it difficult to trust God's plan?

Joshua and Caleb spoke out against the rest of the Israelites. What was the result of their brave behavior?

ISRAEL'S REFUSAL TO ENTER THE LAND (1:19–33)

Moses recounts the rebellion among the people after the twelve spies had reported on their exploration of the Promised Land.

THE PENALTY FOR ISRAEL'S REBELLION (1:34–46)

Their fearful reaction to the native inhabitants of the Promised Land had caused rebellion among the Israelites. Because of their faithful reporting, only Joshua and Caleb are given the promise to one day enter Canaan.

THE WILDERNESS YEARS (2:1–25)

Moses further recounts how God had directed the people to pass through the land around Mount Seir. They could not inhabit this land promised to Esau's descendants, but they did purchase food and water for their journey through the wilderness.

What price did King Sihon and his people pay for their sinful refusal to let Israel pass through their land? How do we resist God's plans?

THE DEFEAT OF KING SIHON (2:26–37)

Further, Moses tells how King Sihon had refused safe passage through Heshbon. At God's direction, the Israelites had destroyed every city, man, woman, and child, keeping only the livestock for themselves.

 CLEAR THE CONFUSION

Why does God declare that certain people are "devoted to destruction"?

Because of King Sihon's sinful stubbornness, God uses the Israelites to completely annihilate the people of Heshbon. The Israelites captured all the cities as they wiped out everything except the livestock. God used the Israelites as tools of His judgment, for a brief time and at His command, to enact His wrath against sin. This destruction foreshadows the ultimate destruction of all people who deserve God's wrath against their sins.

We, too, deserve to be devoted to destruction for our sin, but Jesus took that punishment upon Himself for our sake. Jesus experienced God's wrath in our place so that those who believe in Him will not suffer God's eternal judgment. Through Christ, we become God's chosen ones.

The Defeat of King Og (3:1–22)

Like Sihon before him, Og of Bashan had refused safe passage to the people. The Israelites had captured sixty walled cities, wiping out the entire population of Bashan. Once again, the livestock and riches of Bashan had become spoils of war for Israel.

 CLEAR THE CONFUSION

What are "spoils of war"?

The practice of taking the valuables from a defeated enemy is referred to as the "spoils of war." At God's direction, the Israelites take the livestock and wealth from each of the peoples they defeated as they journeyed toward the Promised Land. These spoils would help them establish themselves as they settled into the Promised Land.

 VISUALIZE

Spoils of War

The Israelites were instructed to take certain material goods from the enemies they defeated. These spoils could include livestock, precious metals and jewels, and grain.

Moses Forbidden to Enter the Land (3:23–29)

Moses once again pleads with God for the privilege to enter the Promised Land. However, God remains firm in His judgment against Moses. God will allow Moses to look across the Jordan to see the land he will never enter.

 Sometimes God answers our prayers with a "NO!" Why is it difficult when God tells you no?

CLEAR THE CONFUSION

Why did God tell Moses to stop asking to lead Israel into the Promised Land?

The consequences for sin don't fade away or disappear with time. God's decree that Moses would not go into the Promised Land when he was unfaithful stood fast (Numbers 20:2–13). Even when Moses prayed to God to lift that punishment, God saw it fitting that Moses would not receive this blessing. Moses' time of leading God's people was at an end, and it was time for leadership to transition to Joshua and the next generation. God did not desert Moses, though, for Moses would receive a greater reward in the fulfillment of His promise of salvation: Jesus. Moses stood in glory with Elijah, talking with Jesus when He was transfigured, glorified, and recognized as the Son of God by the Father in Luke 9:30.

MOSES COMMANDS OBEDIENCE (4:1–14)

Moses reminds the people to keep all of God's commands that they heard from him. They must teach these commands to their children and their children's children.

IDOLATRY FORBIDDEN (4:15–31)

Moses warns the people against creating or worshiping idols. Moses calls God a consuming fire, recalling his encounter with the burning bush and God's appearance on Mount Sinai.

THE LORD ALONE IS GOD (4:32–40)

Moses recalls how God revealed Himself in fire and wonders. From the burning bush to the plagues on Egypt to the Israelites' miraculous escape from Egypt, God has continued to be with His people.

CITIES OF REFUGE (4:41–43)

Moses establishes three cities where those who have unintentionally killed someone may escape to safety.

The concept of cities of refuge was unique to the time. Why do you suppose God provided these locations?

Reviewing the Covenant (4:44–23:14)

 WAYPOINT

Moses' Second Message: Stipulations of the Covenant (4:44–28:68)

What does this text show us?

Moses begins his second message with a review of the giving of the Ten Commandments. This section concludes with the Shema: "Hear, O Israel: The LORD our God, the LORD is one. You shall love the LORD your God with all your heart and with all your soul and with all your might" (6:4–5). These words must be taught to their children and all succeeding generations.

These introductory thoughts are followed by three sections, each dealing with different types of laws: laws regarding life, worship, and celebrations. Then, Moses moves to laws concerning government, justice, and warfare. The final section deals with miscellaneous laws.

What does this text reveal about God's plan of salvation?

While these sections focus on the Law, they help to point us to the Gospel work of Jesus Christ. It may be difficult to see this on first review, but consider how Jesus kept each of these laws as He lived and taught His disciples here on earth. Jesus was perfectly obedient to God's moral law (the Ten Commandments) as well as the civil and ceremonial laws of the ancient Israelites. He fulfilled the Law for us so that we Christians are no longer under the ceremonial and civil laws of Israel. And we are not condemned by the moral law because Jesus paid our penalty on the cross.

What does this text uncover about our identity and calling as God's people today?

God chooses us as His own, like the children of Israel, God's chosen people, but we do not have to obey specific civil and ceremonials laws such as the sacrificial system. We still live under God's moral law, as summarized in the Ten Commandments, yet as His children, we are forgiven through the work of Jesus Christ when we disobey these. The moral law, the Ten Commandments, still serves as a curb, mirror, and guide for Christians today for how we are to live faithfully as God's human creatures.

As you review these chapters, take note of the various laws and how they may apply in our world today.

God gives salvation through His Son, Jesus Christ. In Him, we receive forgiveness for all of the sins we see in this section. Note how God works though Jesus to accomplish all these things.

How can you tell the difference between God's moral law (right and wrong for all people for all time) and the civil and ceremonial laws (government and worship practices exclusively for God's Old Testament people)? Why is it critical for Christians today to understand the difference?

INTRODUCTION TO THE LAW (4:44–49)

As they prepare to enter the Promised Land, the Israelites are reminded by Moses of how they had defeated their enemies.

THE TEN COMMANDMENTS (5:1–33)

Moses recounts his encounter with God on Mount Sinai and the Ten Commandments God gave him there. When the people had heard the sound of the Lord on the mountain, they had responded in fear and awe of God's power.

THE GREATEST COMMANDMENT (6:1–25)

Moses instructs the people in God's commandment to "love the LORD your God with all your heart and with all your soul and with all your might" (6:5). Israelite parents were encouraged to teach these commands to their children in order that the essentials of the faith be passed down from generation to generation. God's command to do so serves as a encouragement to all parents of all time.

As you read this section, consider why God gave such specific directions for passing the faith on from one generation to the next.

🔗 **LINK BETWEEN THE TESTAMENTS**

The Greatest Commandment (Deuteronomy 6:5 → The Gospels)

Moses reminds us of the greatest commandment: "Love the LORD your God with all your heart and with all your soul and with all your might." This commandment appears again in three of the Gospels. The Pharisees quiz Jesus concerning the greatest commandment in Matthew 22:34–38 and Mark 12:28–30. In Luke's Gospel, a similar question leads to Jesus telling the parable of the Good Samaritan (Luke 10:27–37).

A CHOSEN PEOPLE (7:1–26)

Moses warns against intermarrying with the people who currently inhabit Canaan. Likewise, they must tear down the idols to prevent the worship of false gods. God will clear away the enemies of His chosen people before them.

Consider your relationships with others. How might those relationships stand in the way of your relationship with God?

REMEMBER THE LORD YOUR GOD (8:1–20)

Moses warns the people against forgetting the Lord, who brought them out of Egypt and into a land filled with food and water. The Lord has sustained them throughout their time in the wilderness. Moses expresses his concern that the people might quickly forget their God and turn aside to idols.

Not Because of Righteousness (9:1–12)

As the Israelites prepare to cross the Jordan River into the Promised Land, God reminds them that even as their enemies fall before them, it is not because of their own righteousness. Rather, their victory comes from the Lord, who has shown His mercy despite their unfaithfulness.

Why are we tempted to take the credit when things go well in our lives?

 CLEAR THE CONFUSION

Why did Moses remind the people that God was not giving them the Promised Land because of their own righteousness?

Moses gave the Israelites this reminder to highlight that God's grace alone drove their victories and their claim on the Promised Land. Occupying the region were peoples much mightier than they, and even when on their own, the Israelites caused themselves plenty of pain, loss, and trouble by disobeying God at various points. If anything was a credit to them, it was the disasters that befell them and how much they did not deserve what they were about to receive. In His great mercy, however, God preserved His people to make a way for Jesus Christ, who would suffer greatly on account of these failings and so many others to redeem all of humanity.

The Golden Calf (9:13–29)

Moses reminds the people of their continued unfaithfulness in the wilderness. The golden calf was just the beginning of the many times they provoked God to anger. Moses pleaded for God to have mercy on these, His people, whom He brought out of Egypt.

New Tablets of Stone (10:1–11)

Moses continues to remind the people how God had instructed him to make stone tablets, on which He wrote the Ten Commandments for a second time. These tablets are placed in the ark of the covenant, which the Levites carry as the Israelites move from place to place.

VISUALIZE

The New Tablets of the Law

After Moses destroyed the original stone tablets inscribed with the Ten Commandments, God directed him to create a new set of tablets, which were placed in the ark of the covenant.

CIRCUMCISE YOUR HEART (10:12–22)

God had established the covenant of circumcision to set apart Abraham and his descendants as God's chosen people. Now Moses calls upon the people to circumcise their hearts as they put aside their stubborn and rebellious ways.

 CLEAR THE CONFUSION

What does it mean to "circumcise your heart"?

The covenant of circumcision was established with Abraham in Genesis 17:1–14 to set apart God's chosen people. In the New Testament, the Jerusalem Council declared that circumcision was not required for believers; rather, they should avoid practices against God's moral law (as summarized in the Ten Commandments).

Circumcision was the process by which God's people are turned back to Him by means of a visible sign, because by nature, they were rebellious and stubborn. A circumcised heart, therefore, is one that has been turned back to God and responds to His love by faith. We can do our best to circumcise our hearts, but in the end, our sinful nature will thwart us every time. Only Jesus can "create in [us] a clean heart . . . and renew a right spirit within [us]" (Psalm 51:10), by covering us with His righteousness.

In what ways, if any, do these specific blessings and curses apply to God's people today?

LOVE AND SERVE THE LORD (11:1–32)

The children of Israel will face temptation to turn away from God once they experience the plenty found in the Promised Land. Moses encourages the people to teach their children God's words. They face a blessing and a curse—a blessing when they obey God's Word, and a curse when they turn away from Him.

The LORD's Chosen Place of Worship (12:1–28)

God prepares His people for the move into the Promised Land. The first task involves clearing away the idols and false altars. The people must establish a place to worship the true God; there they will offer blood of animals sacrificed to the Lord.

Why do you think God considers removing the idols in the Promised Land a top priority?

 PICTURE OF THE SAVIOR

A Place of Worship

In this section of Deuteronomy, Moses recounts the commands that prescribed very intentional and specific acts of worship for the Israelites when they enter into the Promised Land. Even here, God gives us a preemptive picture of Christ as the unyielding, true Word. It may have been easier for God's people to offer sacrifices wherever they wanted to or to eat meat without first pouring out the blood, but God specified these ways because it was good and right for them to do. Jesus is the Word, as John writes in his Gospel account, and only through Him can we have access to the Father, forgiveness of sins, and life eternal.

 CLEAR THE CONFUSION

Where would God end up placing His name in Israel?

Somewhat cryptically, God reveals through Moses that He will place His name in a specific city in the land that Israel will occupy. The Scriptures later reveal this city as Jerusalem, described to be the place where Israel will gather to worship God and honor Him with sacrifices, tithes, and offerings. This, however, is not the first time we encounter this location. Jerusalem was built upon the location where God had called Abraham to sacrifice Isaac, and had provided a substitute sacrifice, centuries before (Genesis 22:2). In the book of Joshua, we read that the Israelites first established the tabernacle at Shiloh, some twenty miles north of Jerusalem, when they entered the Promised Land. This was not to be the place for God's name, though, because the Philistines utterly destroyed Shiloh in punishment for Israel's idolatry (Jeremiah 7:12–14). God would not formally establish a city in His name until David captured Jerusalem, made it his capitol, and brought the ark into it (2 Samuel 5–6). Solomon later built the temple there, as described in 1 Kings 5–7.

What does God's establishing of a city where He will place His name tell us about God's relationship with His chosen people?

Warning Against Idolatry (12:29–13:18)

The lands the Israelites will soon occupy contain many idols, so God repeats His warning against the temptation to worship these false gods.

God directs severe punishment, including the death penalty, for those who entice believers to worship false gods.

 LINK BETWEEN THE TESTAMENTS

The People of God

In the Old Testament, only the Israelites were known as "the sons of the LORD your God" (14:1). In the New Testament, all Christians are described as members of God's household: "So then you are no longer strangers and aliens, but you are fellow citizens with the saints and members of the household of God" (Ephesians 2:19). All humans are God's creatures, but only those who are called into God's household by grace through faith in God's promises are rightly called God's children.

CLEAN AND UNCLEAN FOOD (14:1–21)

Moses records regulations regarding the food Israelites are allowed to consume. This listing includes land animals, seafood, and fowl.

 CLEAR THE CONFUSION

What is clean and unclean food?

The Old Testament believers followed strict rules concerning the foods they ate. God gave a special vision of unclean food to the apostle Peter in Acts 10:9–16, which encouraged him to share the Gospel with the Gentiles.

TITHES (14:22–29)

God provides His people with the land they need to grow crops and feed their livestock. In return, they give their tithes to support the priests and those in need.

THE SABBATICAL YEAR (15:1–23)

Every seven years, the Israelites are to observe a sabbatical year. During this year, all debts will be forgiven and any slaves owned by Israelites set free. For those who wish to remain slaves voluntarily, Moses provides instructions for piercing the slave's ear as a sign of the relationship.

PASSOVER (16:1–8)

Chapter 16 outlines the procedures for the celebration of special religious festivals. This first section reminds the people of the requirements for Passover, especially the use of unleavened bread.

Why were the dietary laws for the Israelites so specific?

How do your offerings to the church support the ministry today?

Why was the seventh-year sabbatical so important to the Jewish people?

The Scriptures give specific instructions concerning preparations for the Passover. Jesus instituted the Lord's Supper during the celebration of the Passover with His disciples. How can we prepare to receive the Lord's Supper today?

VISUALIZE

Seder Meal

The seder is the modern-day celebration of the Passover meal first observed by the Israelites as they prepared to leave Egypt. A seder is also sometimes celebrated by Christians as a way to better understand Jesus' last supper with His disciples when He established the Sacrament of Holy Communion. The seder plate has six sections (which gives it the appearance of the Star of David), each with a food that serves to remind the people of the first Passover.

Roasted Egg	The egg reminds people of the sacrifices brought to the temple.
Roasted Lamb Shank Bone	This bone represents the perfect lamb sacrificed and eaten by the Israelites before leaving Egypt.
Charoset	A mix of chopped apple, nuts, cinnamon, and wine represents the mortar the Israelites used to build in Egypt.
Maror	A bitter herb such as horseradish is used to remind the people of their bitter lives as slaves in Egypt.
Parsley	The parsley is dipped twice in salt water. The first time reminds the people of the tears they shed in Egypt. The second brings to mind Egypt's army drowning in the Red Sea.
Chezeret	Also representing bitterness, the sixth place is filled with red horseradish or a raw green vegetable, such as lettuce or celery.

What impact would celebrating these particular feasts each year have on Israelites in passing on the faith to future generations? How is this similar to Christian practices today?

Worshiping trees and Asherah poles may seem odd to us. How did these practices reflect worship in the lands Israel would soon occupy?

THE FEAST OF WEEKS (16:9–12)

God instructs the people to celebrate the Feast of Weeks as they celebrate God's generosity by sharing the wealth of the harvest with those in need.

THE FEAST OF BOOTHS (16:13–17)

Following the harvest, the people are commanded to celebrate the weeklong Feast of Booths, where they set up and live in makeshift shelters to remind them of their time in the wilderness. Unlike the Passover and the Feast of Weeks, all people—including foreigners and sojourners—would participate in the Feast of Booths. Israelite males were to celebrate Passover, Weeks, and Booths every year.

JUSTICE (16:18–20)

God establishes a system of justice; the Israelites are to appoint judges and officers for each town. God reminds these leaders of the responsibility to remain impartial in their work.

FORBIDDEN FORMS OF WORSHIP (16:21–17:7)

God warns against planting trees or Asherah poles alongside the altar of God. God wants the Israelites' best, so animals offered must be without blemish. Those who participate in false worship, including worship of the sun or moon, must be put outside of the city gates and stoned to death. (Two witnesses are required to convict someone of false worship.)

 CLEAR THE CONFUSION

How was stoning used as a form of execution?

The practice of execution by stoning is mentioned in both the Old and New Testaments, typically as a punishment for idolatry or adultery. A brutal method of execution, stoning was intended to subject the condemned person to prolonged suffering before death. The size of stones selected were intended to cause pain and injury without bringing on death too quickly. Stoning was conducted in a public place so the condemned person would become an example of the consequences of that particular sin. Sadly, stoning is still legal under Muslim law in certain countries.

LEGAL DECISIONS BY PRIESTS AND JUDGES (17:8–13)

When judges need assistance with making more difficult decisions, they are to turn to the Levitical priests. The priest's judgment is to be final; the people are not allowed to reject or turn away from the declaration.

LAWS CONCERNING ISRAEL'S KINGS (17:14–20)

God establishes a law saying that if the people choose to appoint a king over themselves, they may do so, but this king may not be from the kingdoms they have overthrown. In addition, the king may not own too many horses, have too many wives, or have too much silver and gold. Finally, the king must write his own copy of God's laws.

PROVISION FOR PRIESTS AND LEVITES (18:1–8)

Since priests and Levites have no land or inheritance, the care and feeding of them is left to the rest of the tribes. Meals for these groups come from the food offerings made to God.

ABOMINABLE PRACTICES (18:9–14)

Once again, Moses warns the people against adopting the false worship practices of those who currently inhabit the land God is giving them. Tolerating child sacrifice and cultic practices would certainly lead the people away from the true God.

God had very specific rules for kings who might one day rule over Israel. Why do you suppose God wanted to limit the wealth of Israel's kings?

Consider the cultic practices and sacrifices performed at the time of the exodus. While these might seem extreme, what practices today might be considered equally as evil?

SET THE SCENE

False Worship and Abominable Practices

God warned His followers against the worship of idols and false gods, as well as participating in the ungodly lifestyles of those who inhabited the land God gave His people.

Asherah	These idols were made from carved tree trunks, stone, or even metal posts and represented a sensual Canaanite goddess.
Baal	This god worshiped by the Canaanites was often portrayed as a winged creature with horns. *Baal* was also used as a generic term for a false god.
Molech/ Moloch	This Canaanite or Ammonite god required human sacrifice, most often children. The victims were placed on Molech's outstretched hands and burned over a fire.
Blemished Animals	Because God requires the very best of our offerings, sacrificing blemished animals was considered an abominable practice.
Divination	The ungodly sought information about the future through cultic practices.
Sorcery	Those in pagan lands used magic or cultic practices.

Moses instructed the people to examine the messages of prophets who would come after him. How and why should we evaluate those who claim to bring messages from God?

A New Prophet like Moses (18:15–22)

Moses tells the people that other prophets would come after him. Moses cautions the people to examine the messages of these prophets to discern whether they have come from God.

 PICTURE OF THE SAVIOR

A Prophet like Moses

During one of his last sermons to the Israelites, Moses declared that there would come one prophet greater than him to proclaim God's Word. This prophet would be born of the Jews yet speak directly from the mouth of God with His authority. He would be like Moses—a leader among His people—but one leading in perfect allegiance to God, even unto death on a cross. This prophet is Jesus Christ! He would be a prophet greater than Moses, and He would deliver His people not into a geographic promised land but into a heavenly kingdom, sealing His people—us!—with His precious blood.

Imagine you're a foreigner walking through Israel and you see a city of refuge. After learning what it is, what might the existence of this city communicate to you about Israel's God and life within the community of His people?

Laws Concerning Cities of Refuge (19:1–13)

Moses explains the purpose of the cities of refuge in greater detail. These cities, scattered throughout the nation, will serve as safe havens for those who accidentally, or without malice, kill someone. However, those who attempt to hide in a city of refuge after intentionally killing someone would be turned over for trial and retribution.

Property Boundaries (19:14)

God protects the right of individuals to own property by declaring that it is illegal to move the boundary markers on an individual's land.

Property Markers

In biblical times, property owners would use markers to indicate the boundaries of their land. Such boundary markers have continued to be used over the years. Boundary markers may have been stone posts carved with the property owner's name. Some markers were simply wooden or metal posts to indicate the corners of the land.

LAWS CONCERNING WITNESSES (19:15–21)

In order to convict someone accused of a crime, two or more witnesses must give matching testimony against the accused. All witnesses must appear before the priests and the judges. Those who testify falsely will face the same punishment as the accused.

What might the need for multiple witnesses show us about God's justice?

LAWS CONCERNING WARFARE (20:1–20)

The Lord outlines the rules of engagement as the Israelites prepare to enter the Promised Land. God assures them not to fear when facing armies who seem greater than their army. Initially, the people are to offer a peaceful solution, but if none can be reached, they must take the land forcibly. The Lord outlines provisions for those who should be excused from service in the army due to their life circumstances.

God desires a peaceful resolution to conflict, but when that is not possible, He allows His people to serve in the military. How can we serve our Lord and our nation?

CLEAR THE CONFUSION

Why Did Moses Seek Peaceful Resolution?

God desires for His people to live in peace and harmony with fellow believers and also those outside of the family of faith. God instructed His people to avoid conflict with the inhabitants of certain areas as they passed through on the route to the Promised Land. Some of these foreign kings ignored this request for peaceful passage and suffered destruction as a result.

ATONEMENT FOR UNSOLVED MURDERS (21:1–9)

The Scriptures outline the process for making atonement when a murder cannot be solved. A prescribed sacrifice is performed in order to offer repentance, even if the perpetrator remains unknown.

MARRYING FEMALE CAPTIVES (21:10–14)

When a Jewish man falls in love with a female captured in war, he must first shave her head and allow for a time of mourning before he can take her to be his wife. There are also provisions for peaceable divorce if the marriage does not work. Though unusual in modern terms, these rules for marrying captives helped to protect these female captives from abuse typically endured in cultures of the day.

God makes provisions for the firstborn son in families, whether loved or unloved. How does this affect the relationship between parents and children?

INHERITANCE RIGHTS OF THE FIRSTBORN (21:15–17)

Even if the firstborn son is born to an unloved wife, he is still entitled to a double portion of the estate.

A REBELLIOUS SON (21:18–21)

If a son is rebellious and disobedient, his parents are allowed to take him to the city elders. The leaders of the city are directed to put this rebellious young man to death by stoning.

 LINK BETWEEN THE TESTAMENTS

A Rebellious Son (Deuteronomy 21 → Luke 15)

In Luke 15:11–32, Jesus told the parable of the prodigal son. The account of the father's loving response to the rebellious son stands in stark contrast to the rules outlined in Deuteronomy. We see this in our heavenly Father's grace, demonstrated through Jesus' death and resurrection.

A Man Hanged on a Tree Is Cursed (21:22–23)

 WAYPOINT

What does this text show us?

Once convicted criminals were executed, their bodies were to be hanged on a tree or impaled on a pole. The body was displayed to demonstrate that justice had been done. This section of Deuteronomy reminds the people to remove the body and not leave it exposed overnight.

What does this text reveal about God's plan of salvation?

The cursed one who will hang upon the tree is Jesus, our Savior from sin. Through His innocent life, false conviction, crucifixion on the cross, and glorious resurrection, we have eternal life with Him.

What does this text uncover about our identity and calling as God's people today?

Jesus has taken the curse of the cross on our behalf. As His chosen ones, we can live for Him and share the joy that the curse of sin has been removed through Christ.

 **PICTURE OF THE SAVIOR**

Man Hanged on a Tree Is Cursed

While Moses continued to explain the civil law God had given to Israel, he made a remark that brings us right to the feet of Jesus on the cross. The provision for executed criminals was a brutal hanging on a tree and burial the same day, for they are cursed by God and would defile the holy land God had set aside for Israel. A greater gift was yet to come in His Son, who would also be hanged on a tree and cursed for our iniquities. Jesus suffered the penalty of the Law so that we are hallowed by His righteousness and redeemed to the Father in heaven.

The practice of displaying the bodies of those executed served as another reminder of the consequences of breaking the law. How did Jesus' crucifixion reflect this same practice?

Skim through this text as well as the Passion account (Luke 23). Where do you see similarities?

In Christ, we have a new beginning. Describe the ways God has changed the curse of sin into the promise of salvation for all who call on Him as Lord and Savior.

DEUTERONOMY

Various Laws (22:1–12)

The Lord provides laws dealing with a number of minor issues. Interestingly, many of these laws provide positive directions rather than prohibited behaviors. This positive focus helps the Israelites understand and live in community with one another.

Laws Concerning Sexual Immorality (22:13–30)

The frank discussion of virginity and sexual activity might surprise some readers. The importance of a virgin bride in Jewish society serves as one of the reasons for these very specific laws dealing with engagement, betrothal, and marriage. Sexual purity is highly valued for both men and women in a marriage relationship.

God desires sexual purity among His followers. Why is it important for Christians to remain sexually pure?

What parallels do you see between marriage in biblical times and marriage today? What differences do you see?

 SET THE SCENE

Marriage in Biblical Times

During biblical times, there were three distinct stages to getting married:

Engagement: Parents arranged the engagement when the individuals were very young.

Betrothal: When the young woman reached puberty, she still lived in her father's household for about a year.

Marriage: The couple made their public vows of marriage and began living together.

 LINK BETWEEN THE TESTAMENTS

Consequences of Unplanned Pregnancy → Mary (Deuteronomy 22:20–21 → Matthew 1:18–25)

The laws given to Moses spell out the severe consequences of sexual impurity for young women. Mary, the mother of our Lord Jesus, faced these potential consequences when she found herself pregnant while betrothed but not yet married to Joseph. Blessedly, Joseph decided not to publicly humiliate Mary, and after his encounter with the angel, he took Mary as his wife and became the earthy father of our heavenly Savior.

THOSE EXCLUDED FROM THE ASSEMBLY (23:1–8)

The Lord prohibits emasculated men, those born out of wedlock, and those descended from Moab and Ammon from being part of the assembly. Only those descendants of Israel, Esau, and those who came out of Egypt were allowed to participate.

UNCLEANNESS IN THE CAMP (23:9–14)

Moses lays out the very practical rules regarding basic sanitation when dealing with bodily functions.

Miscellaneous Laws (23:15–28:68)

The arrangement of the miscellaneous laws in the following chapters may seem somewhat disordered. Moses obviously had a purpose for the order in which he listed these laws, but the reasoning has been lost through the ages.

 LINK BETWEEN THE TESTAMENTS

God's Law as a Ward against the Devil → Jesus' Defense against Temptation (Deuteronomy 6, 8 → Matthew 4 and parallels)

But [Jesus] answered, "It is written, 'Man shall not live by bread alone, but by every word that comes from the mouth of God.'" (Matthew 4:4)
Jesus said to him, "Again it is written, 'You shall not put the Lord your God to the test.'" (Matthew 4:7)
Then Jesus said to him, "Be gone, Satan! For it is written, 'You shall worship the Lord your God and Him only shall you serve.'" (Matthew 4:10)

The "second law" of Moses' last book, Deuteronomy, recaptured the covenant God made with His people atop Mount Sinai. Beyond that, it would serve as a lasting reminder of the importance of His Law for all believers through the example of Jesus' temptation. In the sweltering desert, how else does Jesus resist Satan's traps and lies than with the unflinching truth of God's Law?

Indeed, Jesus' responses to Satan all come from Deuteronomy (8:3; 6:16; 6:13), illustrating that even while the Law itself is powerless to save sinners and was given to the Israelites long ago, it shows us our need for a Savior and is useful as a guide and ward against evil in our lives, right here and right now. Only by Jesus' perfect obedience to the Law, His innocent suffering and atoning death, and His glorious resurrection could we be saved from the wrath of God revealed in the Ten Commandments.

Not everyone was allowed into the assembly. Why do you suppose God excluded these individuals?

The fact that God was concerned about the practical matters of camp sanitation shows His concern for even the small details. What does this teach us about God's concern for all the details of our lives?

MISCELLANEOUS LAWS (23:15–25)

The laws in this section deal with respecting the personal property of others, financial matters, the sinful worship practices of foreign gods, and caring for the needs of others. These laws help guide the Israelites as they live in community with one another.

God outlines very specific guidelines for divorce and remarriage. How can we apply these guidelines in the world today?

LAWS CONCERNING DIVORCE (24:1–4)

If a man divorces his wife and sends her away, and then she marries another man but that man dies or divorces her, the first husband is not allowed to marry her again. Interestingly, this section does not deal with the general rules concerning divorce, only the very specific instance of a man remarrying a wife.

MISCELLANEOUS LAWS (24:5–25:4)

In addition to laws concerning newly married men and leprosy, we find a number of rules that show respect to those with financial difficulties. These laws ensure the fair treatment of individuals while preventing wealthier individuals from taking advantage of other people's poverty. If the court finds a man guilty of a crime deserving beating, he cannot be flogged more than forty times.

 LINK BETWEEN THE TESTAMENTS

Corporal Punishment (Deuteronomy 25:1–3 → 2 Corinthians 11:24)

Old Testament Jewish law placed a limit of forty lashes for a convicted criminal. Later, the limit changed to thirty-nine lashes, which Paul suffered at least five times, according to 2 Corinthians 11:24.

While men are no longer required to marry a brother's widow, how can we care for those who have lost a spouse?

LAWS CONCERNING LEVIRATE MARRIAGE (25:5–10)

The term *levirate* comes from the Latin *levir*, meaning "brother-in-law." If a man dies without a son to inherit his property, the law requires the man's brother to take the widow as his own wife. This practice ensures that the woman will be cared for throughout her life.

 CLEAR THE CONFUSION

What was the importance of levirate marriage in ancient Israel?

Levirate marriage was important for keeping family lines alive in the event that a husband died in work or war so that the Israelite people could persist as a strong and healthy nation. A widow could marry her husband's brother and bear a son from him that would carry on the name of her dead husband.

The husband's brother could refuse, but his line would then be cast out of Israel's books instead. This practice secured the proliferation of family lines, as well as property rights, through Israel's history and became a reminder of the promise to Abraham of numerous descendants.

 LINK BETWEEN THE TESTAMENTS

Levirate Marriage and the Sadducees (Deuteronomy 25:5–10 → Matthew 22:23–33)

In Matthew's Gospel, the Sadducees used questions concerning the law of levirate marriage in an attempt to trick Jesus. The imaginary situation presented by the Sadducees concerned a woman who married seven brothers in succession, each of whom died without leaving a son. They wanted to know whose wife she will be in the resurrection. Their question reflected their doubts concerning the resurrection and their lack of faith. Jesus chastised them for their lack of understanding of the Scriptures and the power of God.

MISCELLANEOUS LAWS (25:11–19)

The laws in this section deal with physical disputes, fair and trustworthy measures when conducting business, and God's promised rest when they defeat their enemies.

OFFERINGS OF FIRSTFRUITS AND TITHES (26:1–19)

Every year, the Israelites are to gather one tenth of their crops and take them to the place God commanded as a thanksgiving for His rescue from slavery in Egypt. Every third year, the offering will remain in the local community to help provide for those in need. The chapter concludes by reminding the people to remain faithful to God's commands.

God provided guidelines for giving gifts from their harvest. You may not harvest grain, but how can you share your firstfruits with God?

THE ALTAR ON MOUNT EBAL (27:1–8)

Mount Ebal lies between the Jordan River and the Mediterranean near the city of Shechem in Canaan. God commands the people to build an altar here from field stones covered in plaster. On the altar, they must record the words of the Law given to Moses by God.

How is the altar in your church similar to or different from the altar God described for Mount Ebal?

CURSES FROM MOUNT EBAL (27:9–26)

Moses and the priests instruct the people concerning God's plan as the people enter the Promised Land. On Mount Ebal, the priests will declare curses against those who defy God's Law as the people respond, "Amen!"

Knowing God's plan for our salvation, how should we be living our everyday lives?

BLESSINGS FOR OBEDIENCE (28:1–14)

God promises blessings to those who remain faithful to His laws. While we cannot keep the Law perfectly, these words guide us toward the behavior God desires of us.

CURSES OF DISOBEDIENCE (28:15–68)

The list of curses for disobeying God's Law far outnumbers the list of blessings listed earlier in this chapter. Given the Israelites' history of disobedience while traveling through the wilderness for forty years, God's message should not surprise us. Like the disobedient Israelites, we deserve nothing but God's wrath and punishment. But He gives us His own Son as the perfect sacrifice for our sins.

Renewing the Covenant (29:1–30:20)

 WAYPOINT

Moses' Third Message: God's Covenant Renewed (29:1–30:20)

What does this text show us?
Moses warns the people against disobedience and encourages the people to obey the Lord and His Commandments. Finally, Moses calls on the people to make a choice between good and evil.

What does this text reveal about God's plan of salvation?
The text lays out God's plan for repentance and forgiveness, which—while directed at the Israelites—applies directly to God's people today.

What does this text uncover about our identity and calling as God's people today?
In this section, we see the day-to-day life of the Christian played out as we seek God's forgiveness and hear the wonderful message of absolution. Through this process of confession and absolution, we live out our various callings as God's people.

As you read these final chapters of Deuteronomy, how do you hear the urgency in Moses' message?

Where do we see repentance and forgiveness carried out in the life of the Christian Church?

How can we love and serve others as we live out our lives?

THE COVENANT RENEWED IN MOAB (29:1–29)

Moses assembles the people to recount everything God has done—from bringing them out Egypt through the forty years in the wilderness to the brink of the Jordan. Those waiting to enter the Promised Land were under the age of twenty when they left Egypt, so this message serves to remind them of God's mighty works.

REPENTANCE AND FORGIVENESS (30:1–10)

God reminds the Israelites of the importance of repentance. The Lord reminds the people of the blessings that come from repentance and forgiveness. As they settle into the Promised Land, God will prosper His people as they grow in both number and wealth.

THE CHOICE OF LIFE AND DEATH (30:11–20)

The Israelites find themselves with a challenge: do they remain faithful to the Lord, who has brought them into the Promised Land, or do they turn aside to the false gods from the lands they will occupy? Their decision is literally one that leads to life or death.

What important statements, words, or phrases stick out to you most from this section? Why?

Leadership Succession (31:1–34:12)

JOSHUA TO SUCCEED MOSES (31:1–8)

 WAYPOINT

What does this text show us?
Moses has worked hard over the last forty years to lead God's people out of bondage and through the wilderness to the edge of the Promised Land. He is now 120 years old. Before he dies, he brings forward Joshua, his longtime assistant, who will take his place leading God's people. Joshua has been serving Moses from early on, commanding the military, accompanying Moses to Mount Sinai, and spying on Canaan. Now God appoints, or commissions, Joshua to lead His people into the Promised Land, where Joshua is commanded to either drive out or destroy the peoples who live there.

What are some similarities and differences that you see between the work of Joshua and of Jesus, the greater Joshua, who would come one day to die for the sins of the world?

What does this text reveal about God's plan of salvation?
Joshua is a striking figure in the period of the exodus. He is God's chosen commander, who will lead God's people through the Jordan River into the Promised Land, defeating their enemies. Some 1,500 years later, the angel Gabriel appeared to Mary, announcing the coming Messiah and giving her the name the child would be called. Though we know His name as *Jesus*, which is the Greek version of the name, His name in Hebrew is *Joshua*. His parents and community likely called Him Joshua growing up. This God-given name means "God saves." Joshua's task in the Old Testament foreshadows Jesus, the new Joshua, and His greater task in the New Testament.

How does Jesus work as a warrior and commander? What impact does that have on your life?

Think about other places where leadership is passed from one person to another. How can we trust God to guide that process?

What does this text uncover about our identity and calling as God's people today?

It's easy to think of Jesus' life and ministry as only that of a messenger, but like Joshua, He is also a warrior and commander. As such, He leads God's people today, and we follow where He leads us. We listen to His command and communication, that is, God's Word; we gather together to receive His gifts with fellow Christians in worship; and we strive to live out our baptismal identities in Christ in our various roles, including at home, at work, in society, and in the congregation.

 PICTURE OF THE SAVIOR

Prophet, Priest, and King

Moses served as prophet, priest, and king for the Israelites as they escaped slavery in Egypt, made their way through the wilderness, and prepared to enter the Promised Land.

Jesus Christ, our Prophet (Luke 4:18–19), Priest (Hebrews 7:26–27), and King (1 Timothy 6:14–16), brings us out of our slavery to sin and into the promised land of eternal life with Him.

How can we share the message of God's plan of salvation with others who do not know Him?

THE READING OF THE LAW (31:9–13)

Moses records another copy of God's Law, which is given to the priests. Every seven years, at the Feast of Booths, the priests must read the Law to the people.

JOSHUA COMMISSIONED TO LEAD ISRAEL (31:14–29)

As Moses' days on earth draw to a close, he and Joshua enter the tabernacle to meet with the Lord. God commissions Joshua to take over the leadership of the people as Moses prepares a farewell message for the people.

Think about a favorite hymn. How does that hymn recount the story of Christ and His work in our lives?

THE SONG OF MOSES (31:30–32:47)

Moses composes a song that recounts the history of God's people, beginning with God's call to Abraham. Throughout their history, the people had strayed from God's Law and worshiped idols. Moses warns them against this foolish behavior and recounts God's promise to be with and care for His people as they enter the Promised Land.

MOSES' DEATH FORETOLD (32:48–52)

God directs Moses to ascend Mount Nebo and gaze upon the Promised Land, which he will not experience. Like his brother, Aaron, before him, Moses will be "gathered to his people" (v. 50) in death before the Israelites enter the land God first promised to Abraham.

MOSES' FINAL BLESSING ON ISRAEL (33:1–29)

Moses offers one last blessing to all the people. His blessing is broken into sections, with each section dedicated to one of the tribes of Israel. These blessings include events that won't occur until after Israel occupies the Promised Land.

THE DEATH OF MOSES (34:1–12)

 WAYPOINT

What does this text show us?
God shows Moses all of the Promised Land from his viewpoint atop Mount Nebo. There, Moses dies, and the people mourn his death for thirty days. At the end of their time of mourning, Joshua assumes the role of leader over God's people.

What does this text reveal about God's plan of salvation?
God had sent His servant Moses, who spent forty years leading God's people through the wilderness to the brink of the Promised Land. One day God would send His own Son to lead all people to the promised land of heaven. Through His death and resurrection, this new heaven and new earth will be theirs for all eternity.

What does this text uncover about our identity and calling as God's people today?
Just as God had a plan to rescue His people and bring them into the Promised Land, He has a plan to rescue us and bring us to our eternal promised land through the death and resurrection of Jesus Christ.

As you read the text, picture in your mind what this scene might have looked like. What stands out to you? Why?

In what ways is Moses' life and ministry similar to and different from Jesus' later, greater life and ministry?

Why is a time of mourning at the loss of a loved one important? Why is it even more important to move on after a time of mourning?

175

CLEAR THE CONFUSION

How did God bury Moses?

When Moses had finished his work after a long and undimmed life, God laid him to rest in a loving and merciful manner. Before Moses died, God took him up to the top of Mount Nebo and showed him the land first promised to Abraham all those years ago. Even though Moses would not be allowed to lead Israel into the Promised Land himself, God gave him the assurance that the Israelites would have this new home. Furthermore, God buried Moses in such a way that his burial site remains unknown—another blessing from God. His enemies would not be able to defile his body, nor would his descendants worship him instead of God, whom he served.